Y0-CAX-688

Shall We Gather

Recipes and Remembrances of a River Town

Shall We Gather

Recipes and Remembrances of a River Town

Published by
The Church Ladies of Trinity Episcopal Church
5375 U.S. Hwy 231
Wetumpka, AL 36092
334-567-7534

This cookbook is a collection of favorite recipes,
which are not necessarily original recipes.

Library of Congress Control Number: 2007901414
ISBN: 978-0-9792589-0-9

Edited, Designed, and Manufactured by
Favorite Recipes® Press
An imprint of

FRP

P. O. Box 305142
Nashville, Tennessee 37230
800-358-0560

Art Director: Steve Newman
Book Design: Jim Scott
Project Editor: Cathy Ropp

Manufactured in China
First Printing 2007
6,000 copies

To order additional copies see page 192.

Table of Contents

Foreword 4
Artist Biography 5
Introduction 6
Dedications 7

Appetizers and Beverages 10
Soups and Salads 30
Breakfasts and Breads 52
Beef and Pork Main Dishes 72
Poultry Main Dishes 90
Seafood Main Dishes 106
Vegetables and Side Dishes 126
Desserts 148

Contributors 182
Sponsors 184
Index 186
Order Information 192

Foreword

"Anybody with enough money can build a dream house," a southern woman once told me, "But no matter how beautiful it is, and no matter how many rooms it's got, it'll be just like any other house, big or small, because it won't become a home until it's filled with cooking smells."

I could not agree more. If, upon walking into a house, I am greeted by the seductive aroma of a pot roast or a cherry pie, I hardly notice the dècor. The olfactory evidence of a beef and okra stew or a barbecue will make me feel right at home no matter how humble the abode. Let the upholstery be frayed, the paint peeling, the doors hanging askew. Who cares? There's going to be something wonderful to eat.

At least, it may seem that way at first whiff. The proof, of course, is always in the eating. Some people have better luck than others at making food come out right—the cook's version of a green thumb, I guess—and they become known in the community for one or more of their dishes. That's the beauty of the book you hold in your hand. These are the recipes that have turned out right, time and time again.

Better still, they are offered up by people you know and trust. And this is important, because it is a fact that famous restaurant chefs who write cookbooks often leave important ingredients out of their recipes so their competitors won't be able to duplicate their signature dishes. And neither will you. Although I haven't had the pleasure of meeting the lady, I'm pretty sure Ruth Stovall isn't going to pull that sort of trick on you. Neither is Janette Belcher, or Katyleene Kendall, or Shirley Eberhart, or Bessie Brand.

Southern food is comfort food. It makes you feel good. It is appetizingly heaped on a plate, not arranged in a neat "tower" or some other sculptural form. Gravy, if there is any, is generously poured on top—not "drizzled" or drawn on the plate in swirls and dots like a piece of modern art.

With few exceptions, the recipes are designed for people who have plenty else to do besides cook—they are easy to make. The ingredients are commonly available; you won't have to go scouting around for eye of newt. I also notice a tilt toward healthful food—there is not one deep-fried mouthful in the whole book, and while the fat content is high enough to delight the taste buds, it's considerably lower than the old-style coronary-attack levels. Still, given where the recipes come from, I am not surprised to find that the greatest selection of recipes by far are desserts—Southern Tea Cakes, Bette's Chocolate Sheet Cake, Cold Apple Pie, and Alabama Banana Pudding.

Like most home-town cookbooks, the *Shall We Gather* cookbook has a distinctive personality. It reveals a lot about Wetumpka, especially the cooking smells that greet you when you walk in the door.

—John Berendt
Author of *Midnight in the Garden of Good and Evil* and *City of Falling Angels*

Artist Biography

Cover artist Hope Brannon, award-winning artist and art educator, has deep roots in Wetumpka. She attended Huntingdon College, graduated from Auburn University in Montgomery and has a Master of Art Education degree from Troy University. She teaches art at The Montgomery Academy and is a member of Trinity Parish.

Copies of the cover art are available through ***www.trinitywetumpka.org/cookbook***.

Introduction

Wetumpka is graced by three beautiful pre-Civil War churches. The Methodist, Baptist and Presbyterian congregations worship in marvelous historical buildings, worthy of any visitor's time and scrutiny. But no one has a building more tied to local history than Trinity Episcopal Church.

A group convened in 1947 for the purpose of establishing a new church, as an Episcopal parish had not existed in Wetumpka for nearly one hundred years. Only six families were represented, a total of thirteen individuals. But from this small beginning a lively parish grew.

By the late 1960s, the small parish had outgrown its original home on Austin Lane. Dr. J. E. (Beau) Dunn, Jr., knew the old Cantelou-Law cotton warehouse on the banks of the Coosa was to be demolished, so Beau and Ebba Dunn bought our current church building. The parish paid for it to be transported to its current location and converted it into beautiful worship space.

Admiral Henry Crommelin and Captain Quentin Crommelin generously provided land once owned by the wealthy Creek planter Alexander McGillivray as a new location. The rest is history.

Our Rector, The Reverend Bennett Alford, Jr., is from a family with a long history in the cotton business. When Ben entered the church for the first time, he recognized the clean, unmistakable smell of cotton.

We are a parish steeped in history and tradition, but very much looking to the future. Wetumpka is county seat to one of the fastest growing counties in Alabama. Now 40,000 cars a day pass in front of our church on U.S. Highway 231. Our charming and well-loved cotton warehouse is bursting at the seams. We are growing in number and we must grow in space.

We want to provide a place for God's people to gather, worship, pray, learn, and teach, as well as to play, love, and support each other. It would be comfortable to remain a small church, but we believe that God has bigger plans for us.

This book is dedicated to the Glory of God and the mission and ministry of Trinity Episcopal Church.

We invite you to worship with us.

Dedications

Harriet Landrum, for my daughters Elizabeth Michalets and Slater Rowlett.

In loving memory of Ettra Spencer Seay, Sine Qua Non

Judie Hooks and Leslie Mattox honor the memory of Lucile Kennedy who taught us the spices of life.

To honor Aunt Jenny for all her love, kindness, and understanding, by the Searcys and the Catons.

To my family, Trey, Parker, and Patrick Lackey, by Charlotte Lackey.

In loving memory of our friends, Janet and Ben Barrett, by Mike and Becky Bannon.

Voncille Lankford, in memory of Burnley H. Lankford who loved good food.

In memory of Uncle David Dixon and Aunt Mary Ellen Dixon, and to honor friends Janette and Ed Chalker, by Andrea Miller.

Pam Stein wishes to honor Mary Ann Neeley, the grand lady of many a river gathering!

Warren Sez—To Hazel Jones, the author of good food!

In honor of my mother, Ann Jeter, retired Florida extension agent, who created many recipes enjoyed by family and friends, by Belyn Richardson.

Dedication and thanks to the cookbook committee for all their hard work.

In appreciation of Jim Richardson, my favorite cook, from his wife, Belyn

Barbara Davis honors the men who light up her life and grill, Mike, Jake, and Hamp.

Dedications

In appreciation for Allison and Laura Chambliss and the many meals they prepare for my sons and grandsons, Baker, Ben, Bake, and William.

With love to Phyllis Kennedy, whose meals are the best—Crawford.

Becky Wilkinson dedicates this cookbook to the best two cooks in the world, my daughter Shauna Baker, and my sister Barbara Caughlin.

To the three people in my life that love everything I cook, my granddaughters Ashley, Emily, and Riley Baker.

Phil Holland and family honor Jimmy and Carol Holland.

In honor of Eunice Alford and in memory of Bennett Alford, Evelyn Dugan, and Laurence Dugan by Ben and Lynn Alford.

In memory of Gladys Cowart Howell, one of the world's greatest cooks, by Ray Howell.

In loving memory of my wife Florence Christie Ford, by Colonel Thomas S. Ford.

In memory of Mary Maddox, an exceptional cook, hostess, and sister, by Rebecca Gregory.

In honor of Katyleene S. Kendall (Mother) and Ruth Stovall (Aunt), by Dr. Julius (Beau) and Mary Elizabeth (Ebba) Dunn.

In loving memory of my husband Conrad "Connie" J. Ward, by June Ward.

In thanksgiving for Phyllis Kelly Kennedy for her dedication and direction of the Shall We Gather *cookbook, by June Ward.*

Dedications

In honor of my mother Sherrell Hardin Waddle for teaching me to love cooking, with love Virginia Waddle Lott.

Crawford and Phyllis honor the memory of Ma, Pipe Rat, Conrad, and Brad.

Perry Elizabeth and Kevin Caton, Bayne, Melissa, Baylor, and Owen Searcy, with all our love Mamie and Paw Paw.

In memory of Eva Grace Waltman, Amy W. Jones and Warren L. Jones, III, for the best seafood gumbo ever!

With love to Crawford, the most appreciative audience a cook ever had, by P. K. K.

Phyllis Kennedy dedicates this book to Leah and Paula, the A-Team in cooking.

Phyllis and Crawford Kennedy honor the memory of Brad who loved his Mama's cooking.

This book is dedicated to the memory of Bruce Kelly who even now enabled its success.

The cookbook committee offers a loving tribute to Virginia Lott who dropped from heaven.

With love and appreciation to June Ward for all those good dinners, P. C. J.

Phyllis Kennedy dedicates: SWG *to my mother Virginia Kelly and grandmothers Mama Ree and Ma Kelly who made me want to know how to cook.*

Love and gratitude to the cookbook committee who shared laughs, cooked, tasted, butted heads, and bonded to bring this book to life.

SUMP'N'S A COMIN'

In the early 1800s, folks gathered on the banks of the Coosa River to watch the riverboats dock in Wetumpka. The rapids upriver made it impossible to navigate further, so the boats that plied the river between Wetumpka and Mobile carried cotton from farms and plantations miles away and brought goods from around the world. This lively commerce led a New York newspaper to report in 1836 "Wetumpka, Alabama, and Chicago, Illinois, are the most promising two cities of the West."

Wetumpka's central location and importance in the cotton economy resulted in the city's consideration as the site for Alabama's capital. The major competitor was Montgomery. Montgomery's leaders stacked the deck by entertaining state legislators with an elaborate dinner prepared by a French chef in a newly built hotel. After sixteen ballots, Wetumpka lost the capital by one vote.

As cotton's economic importance diminished, Wetumpkans turned to other commercial enterprises. One nineteenth-century entrepreneur was J. M. Jenkins, who lost a leg in a railroad accident. While recuperating, he began to design and build beehives. His design was ingenious and the demand for his hives spread throughout the southeast, but he was unable to find a reliable supply of bricks. He solved his problem by establishing a highly successful brick plant and for a while made both beehives and brick before devoting his energy totally to the production of bricks.

Mr. Jenkins had the distinction of owning the first automobile in Wetumpka. While on his way to the Methodist Church one day, he passed down a residential street where a worker was chopping wood. The man saw the strange buggy and heard the chugging engine. He threw down his axe and ran to the house shouting, "Sump'n's a comin' and they ain't nothing pullin' it!"

This section was generously sponsored by

JENKINS BRICK

Appetizers and Beverages

GATHER YOURSELVES

TOGETHER, YEA,

GATHER TOGETHER.

ZEPHANIAH 2:1

Pickled Black-Eyed Peas

MAKES 8 TO 9 CUPS

2 (15-ounce) cans black-eyed peas, drained
1/2 cup vegetable oil
1/4 cup apple cider vinegar
1/4 cup green olives
1/4 cup sliced onions
1/2 cup chopped green bell pepper
1/2 cup chopped red bell pepper
1 garlic clove, minced
Salt and pepper to taste

Combine the black-eyed peas, oil, vinegar, olives, onions, bell peppers and garlic in a bowl and mix well. Season with salt and pepper. Marinate, covered, until the flavors meld. Serve with tortilla chips or bagel chips. (**NOTE:** *For a variation, substitute roasted red peppers for the raw.)*

Pepper Vodka Tomatoes

SERVES 8

1 pint vine-ripened grape tomatoes
1/2 cup pepper-flavored vodka
3 tablespoons sea salt
1 tablespoon lemon pepper
1 to 2 tablespoons ground red pepper

Poke five or six holes in each tomato with a fork and place in a shallow bowl. Add the vodka and toss until coated. Let stand, covered, for 1 to 2 hours or until marinated to desired taste, tossing occasionally. Combine the salt, lemon pepper and ground red pepper in a bowl and mix well. Serve on the side of the tomatoes. (**NOTE:** *You may make your own flavored vodka by combining 1/2 cup plain vodka and 2 tablespoons cayenne pepper.)*

Party Pecans

Serves 20

$1^1/_4$ pounds pecans
2 tablespoons coarsely chopped rosemary
1 tablespoon butter, melted
2 teaspoons dark brown sugar
2 teaspoons kosher salt
$^1/_2$ teaspoon cayenne pepper

Spread the pecans evenly on a baking sheet. Bake at 350 degrees for 10 minutes or until light golden brown. Combine the rosemary, butter, brown sugar, salt and cayenne pepper in a large bowl and mix well. Add the hot pecans and toss until coated. Serve immediately. (**Note:** *For a variation, you may use skinless peanuts, cashews, Brazil nuts, hazelnuts, walnuts, or whole almonds instead of the pecans or use a mixture of these nuts.)*

Cheese Straws

Make 3 dozen

2 cups all-purpose flour
$^1/_2$ teaspoon baking powder
$^1/_2$ teaspoon salt
$^1/_4$ teaspoon cayenne pepper
1 pound extra-sharp Cheddar cheese, shredded
9 tablespoons butter, melted

Combine the flour, baking powder, salt and cayenne pepper in a bowl and mix well. Add the cheese and butter and mix until the dough comes together. Roll the dough out. Score the top with a fork and cut into strips with a pizza cutter. Pick up the strips with a spatula and arrange on a baking sheet. Bake at 400 degrees for 8 to 10 minutes or until cooked through. Let stand until completely cool. Store in an airtight container.

Zucchini Cheese Squares

Makes 2 dozen

2 cups chopped green onions
2 garlic cloves, finely chopped
1 to 2 tablespoons olive oil
8 eggs
1 pound sharp Cheddar cheese, shredded
10 saltine crackers, crushed
1 cup chopped fresh parsley
1 1/2 tablespoons (or more) dill weed
6 to 8 drops Tabasco sauce
Salt and pepper to taste
1 1/2 pounds zucchini, thinly sliced
Paprika to taste

Sauté the green onions and garlic in the hot olive oil in a skillet until tender. Beat the eggs in a bowl. Add the green onion mixture, cheese, crackers, parsley, dill weed, Tabasco sauce, salt and pepper and mix well. Add the zucchini and mix until combined. Spread in a thin layer in a well-greased 10×15-inch baking dish. Bake at 325 degrees for 30 minutes. Sprinkle with paprika. Let stand until cool. Slice into small squares. (**Note:** *These are great to serve at brunches and cocktail parties.)*

Tomato, Avocado and Goat Cheese Crostini

SERVES 8 TO 10

1 French baguette
1/3 cup olive oil
2 teaspoons minced garlic
2 avocadoes
4 ounces goat cheese, softened
1/4 teaspoon salt
1 1/2 cups (1/4-inch) pieces seeded Roma tomatoes
1/4 cup fresh basil, chopped
2 tablespoons olive oil
1/2 teaspoon salt
1/4 teaspoon pepper
Small fresh basil leaves

Slice the bread diagonally into 1/4-inch-thick slices. Place in a single layer on a baking sheet. Combine 1/3 cup olive oil and the garlic in a bowl and mix well. Brush the bread slices with the olive oil mixture. Bake at 350 degrees for 10 to 15 minutes or until golden brown and crisp. Let stand until completely cool. Store the crostini in an airtight container until ready to assemble. Combine the avocado, goat cheese and 1/4 teaspoon salt in a bowl and blend until smooth. Combine the tomatoes, basil, 2 tablespoons olive oil, 1/2 teaspoon salt and the pepper in a bowl and toss until combined. Spread 1 tablespoon of the avocado mixture on each crostini. Top with some of the tomato mixture. Garnish with small basil leaves.

Making Pesto

When using the food processor to make pesto, make sure that your processor blade is sharp. Chopping basil and other tender greens with a dull blade will bruise the greens, and they will lose their bright green color.

Mozzarella Pesto Bites

MAKES 2 DOZEN

24 diagonally cut baguette slices
Olive oil
6 ounces fresh mozzarella cheese
1/2 cup pesto
24 roasted red bell pepper strips
(approximately 1/2×1 inch in size)

Place the baguette slices on a baking sheet and brush with olive oil. Bake at 375 degrees for 8 to 10 minutes or until golden brown and crisp. Slice the cheese into twelve slices. Cut each slice on the diagonal into two triangles. Spread each baguette slice with some of the pesto. Place one piece of cheese and a red pepper strip on top.

Pork Tenderloin Sandwiches with Herb Mayonnaise

SERVES 10 TO 12

1 (1 1/2-pound) pork tenderloin
3 tablespoons jerk seasoning
1/4 cup olive oil
1/2 cup water
1 cup mayonnaise
2 tablespoons chopped basil
2 tablespoons chopped chives
2 tablespoons chopped rosemary
2 tablespoons chopped thyme
Salt and pepper to taste
10 to 12 Hawaiian bread rolls

Rub the pork with the jerk seasoning. Brown the pork on all sides in the hot olive oil in a Dutch oven. Add the water. Bake at 350 degrees for 30 minutes. Remove from the oven and let stand until cool. Chill, covered, until ready to serve. Combine the mayonnaise, basil, chives, rosemary and thyme in a bowl and mix well. Season with salt and pepper. Slice the pork. Slice the rolls horizontally and arrange the pork on the bottom halves. Spread some of the herb mayonnaise on the top halves and place mayonnaise side down on top of the pork.

Marinated Roast Beef Sandwiches

SERVES 10

1 (5- to 6-pound) sirloin tip or rump roast
1 (16-ounce) bottle Italian salad dressing
1 onion, chopped
1 cup tarragon vinegar
1 (3-ounce) jar capers, drained
1 (4-ounce) jar pimentos
1/4 cup soy sauce
Pita bread or sandwich bread

Place the sirloin on a grill rack and grill until medium-rare. Chill, covered, for 8 to 10 hours. Combine the salad dressing, onion, vinegar, capers, pimentos and soy sauce and mix well. Slice the sirloin very thin across the grain and place in a shallow baking pan. Pour the marinade over the sirloin. Marinate, covered, in the refrigerator for 4 hours. Serve chilled in pita bread or on sandwich bread.

Smoked Salmon Pâté

MAKES 4 CUPS

1 pound smoked sockeye salmon
16 ounces cream cheese, softened
1 cup mayonnaise
1/2 tablespoon Dijon mustard
1/2 tablespoon lemon juice
1 teaspoon dill weed
3 to 4 pinches of pepper

Remove the skin from the salmon and discard. Place the meat in a food processor. Add the cream cheese in small pieces. Add the mayonnaise, Dijon mustard, lemon juice, dill weed and pepper and process until combined. Serve with crackers, bagels or bread.

Hot Crab Dip

SERVES 5

1 (8-ounce) package fresh crab meat, or 2 (6-ounce) cans crab meat, drained
8 ounces cream cheese, softened
2 tablespoons chopped onion
1 tablespoon milk
1/2 teaspoon horseradish
1/4 teaspoon salt
Dash pepper
Sliced almonds
Paprika

Combine the crab meat, cream cheese, onion, milk, horseradish, salt and pepper in a bowl and stir to mix well. Spoon into a baking dish. Sprinkle almonds and paprika on top. Bake at 375 degrees for 15 minutes. Serve with potato chips or stone wheat crackers.

Shrimp Dip

MAKES 4 CUPS

2 pounds cooked shrimp
1/2 cup chili sauce
1/2 cup mayonnaise
1/4 cup lemon juice
1 teaspoon salt
1/4 teaspoon dry mustard

Process the shrimp, chili sauce, mayonnaise, lemon juice, salt and dry mustard in a blender until combined. Serve with crackers.

Layered Shrimp Party Platter

MAKES ABOUT 5 1/2 CUPS

6 green onions, chopped
1 bell pepper, chopped
3 tomatoes, chopped
2 (8-ounce) containers whipped cream cheese
1 1/2 to 2 (12-ounce) bottles cocktail sauce
2 (4-ounce) cans tiny shrimp, drained
8 ounces mozzarella cheese, shredded

Combine the green onions, bell pepper and tomatoes in a bowl and mix well. Layer the cream cheese, cocktail sauce, shrimp and mozzarella cheese in the order listed in a medium serving platter with sides. Sprinkle the green onion mixture on top. Serve with crackers.

Black-Eyed Pea Hummus

MAKES 3 CUPS

1 (16-ounce) package frozen black-eyed peas
or crowder peas
1 cup pecans
1/2 cup (2 ounces) freshly grated Parmesan cheese
15 large basil leaves
1/2 cup fresh parsley
2 garlic cloves, cut into quarters
1 cup (or less) olive oil
Chopped parsley
Chopped basil

Cook the black-eyed peas using the package directions and drain. Set aside 3/4 cup of the cooked peas. Process the remaining black-eyed peas in a food processor until smooth. Add the pecans, cheese, 15 basil leaves, 1/2 cup parsley and garlic and process until combined. Add the olive oil gradually, processing constantly until smooth. Add the reserved black-eyed peas, reserving a few for garnish. Pulse until chunky but well combined. Spoon into a serving bowl and garnish with chopped parsley, chopped basil and the reserved black-eyed peas. Serve with stone wheat crackers.

Caponata

SERVES 10 TO 12

1 large eggplant, cut into cubes (approximately 3 to 4 cups)
1/4 cup (or more) olive oil
2 green bell peppers, chopped
2 onions, chopped
2 garlic cloves, minced
1 (16-ounce) can tomatoes, or 1 package Pomi Italian tomatoes
1 cup green olives, drained and chopped
1 (3- to 4-ounce) jar capers, drained

Sauté the eggplant in the hot olive oil in a skillet until brown. Remove the eggplant to a bowl with a slotted spoon. Add the bell peppers, onions and garlic to the skillet and sauté until tender, adding additional olive oil as needed. Return the eggplant to the skillet. Stir in the tomatoes, olives and capers. Cook on low until thickened, stirring occasionally. Serve at room temperature with crackers or crusty bread.

Vegetable Mold

SERVES 6 TO 8

1 envelope unflavored gelatin
1/4 cup hot water
1/4 cup cold water
2 cups mayonnaise
2 tomatoes, peeled and chopped
1 cucumber, seeded and chopped
1 cup chopped celery
1 small onion, chopped
1 bell pepper, chopped
Salt to taste

Dissolve the gelatin in the hot water in a large heatproof bowl. Stir in the cold water. Add the mayonnaise and blend until smooth. Fold in the tomatoes, cucumber, celery, onion and bell pepper. Season with salt. Spoon into a mold. Chill, covered, in the refrigerator for 8 to 10 hours or until set. Remove from the mold to a serving platter and serve as a salad or with crackers as an appetizer.

Baked Vidalia Onion Dip

SERVES 12

1/4 cup sour cream
8 ounces cream cheese, softened
3 ounces Parmesan cheese, grated
1 or 2 Vidalia onions, chopped
1 teaspoon Worcestershire sauce
2 or 3 drops of Tabasco sauce
Slivered almonds
Crumbled crisp-cooked bacon

Combine the sour cream, cream cheese and Parmesan cheese in a mixing bowl and blend until smooth. Stir in the onion, Worcestershire sauce and Tabasco sauce. Spoon into a 1 1/2-quart baking dish. Bake at 350 degrees for 30 to 40 minutes or until bubbly. Top with almonds and bacon and bake for an additional 10 minutes. Serve with crackers.

Zesty Cream Cheese

SERVES 4 TO 6

8 ounces cream cheese
1/2 cup sun-dried tomato vinaigrette
2 garlic cloves, thinly sliced
6 sprigs fresh thyme, chopped
Leaves of 3 small fresh rosemary sprigs
1 teaspoon cracked black pepper
Grated zest of 1 lemon

Cube the cream cheese into approximately thirty-six pieces and place in a bowl. Add the vinaigrette, garlic, thyme, rosemary, pepper and lemon zest and toss until combined. Spoon into a 9-inch pie plate or a baking dish. Chill, covered, 1 to 24 hours. Serve with crackers, crusty bread or pita chips. (**NOTE:** *If using light cream cheese, spread on a serving plate instead of cutting into cubes. Mix the remaining ingredients and pour over the cream cheese.)*

Olive and Mushroom Cheese Ball

MAKES $1^1/_2$ TO 2 CUPS

24 ounces cream cheese, softened
1 (4-ounce) can mushrooms, drained and finely chopped
1 (6-ounce) can pitted black olives, drained and finely chopped
1 bunch green onions, minced
1 small jar dried beef, finely chopped
Parsley flakes (optional)
Paprika (optional)

Combine the cream cheese, mushrooms, olives, green onions and beef in a bowl and mix well. Shape into a ball and wrap in plastic wrap. Chill until ready to serve. Remove the plastic wrap and roll in parsley flakes or sprinkle with paprika just before serving.

Asheville's Cranberry Orange Cheese Ball

MAKES 2 CUPS

16 ounces cream cheese, softened
1 (11-ounce) can mandarin oranges, drained and crushed
1 cup dried cranberries
1 Red Delicious apple, chopped
1 teaspoon seasoning salt
1 cup chopped pecans

Combine the cream cheese, mandarin oranges, cranberries, apple and seasoning salt in a bowl and mix well. Shape into a ball and roll in the pecans. Wrap in plastic wrap and freeze for 8 to 10 hours. Thaw for 2 hours before serving. Serve with crackers.

Pimento cheese ... called "P'minnuh Cheese: the Pâté of the South" by Kendra Myer for Southern Foodways Alliance. Every cook thinks his or hers is the best. Add minced onion, pickle relish, chili sauce, sliced olives, pecans, or Ro-tel (diced tomatoes with green chiles) to suit your taste, but freshly grated sharp Cheddar cheese is a must. We like it on crackers, celery, sandwiches, and apple slices, and in eggs or hot tomato soup. In fact, there isn't anywhere we don't like it.

Three-Pepper Pimento Cheese

MAKES 4 1/2 CUPS

1 pound sharp Cheddar cheese, shredded
8 ounces cream cheese, softened
1 (14-ounce) jar roasted red bell pepper
1/3 cup (about) good-quality mayonnaise
Tabasco sauce to taste
Freshly ground pepper to taste

Combine the Cheddar cheese, cream cheese and undrained bell pepper in a food processor or mixing bowl and mix just until combined. Stir in enough mayonnaise to achieve a spreading consistency. Season with Tabasco sauce and pepper.

Monterey Jack and Cheddar Salsa

MAKES 3 CUPS

18 ounces Monterey Jack and Cheddar cheese blend, shredded
1 tomato, chopped
4 green onions, chopped
1 (4-ounce) can chopped green chiles
1/2 cup Italian salad dressing
1 (3-ounce) can chopped black olives
1/4 cup chopped fresh cilantro

Combine the cheese blend, tomato, green onions, green chiles, salad dressing, olives and cilantro in a bowl and mix well. Serve with blue and yellow corn tortilla chips.

Tomato Salsa

MAKES 5 CUPS

12 tomatoes, chopped, or 3 (28-ounce) cans whole tomatoes, drained and chopped
6 to 10 jalapeño chile slices
1 (3-ounce) can black olives
1 teaspoon garlic powder, or 1 garlic glove, crushed
1 teaspoon chili powder
4 green onions

Combine the tomatoes, jalapeño chile, olives, garlic powder, chili powder and green onions in a food processor and pulse until chunky. Serve with chips.

Peach Salsa

SERVES 6 TO 8

1 large garlic clove
1 teaspoon salt
6 peaches, peeled and chopped
1/4 to 1/2 cup chopped cilantro
3 green onions, finely chopped
1 jalapeño chile, seeded and finely chopped
Juice of 1 lime
1 to 2 teaspoons (or more) olive oil
1/2 teaspoon cumin (optional)

Mash the garlic and salt to a paste consistency. Combine the garlic mixture, peaches, cilantro, green onions, jalapeño chile, lime juice, olive oil and cumin in a bowl and mix well. Serve with lime-flavored tortilla chips.

Spiced Cranberry Cider

SERVE 8

1 quart apple cider
3 cups cranberry juice
2 to 3 tablespoons brown sugar
1 (3-inch-long) cinnamon stick
3/4 teaspoon whole cloves
1/2 lemon, thinly sliced

Combine the apple cider, cranberry juice, brown sugar, cinnamon stick, cloves, and lemon slices in a large heavy saucepan. Simmer for 15 to 20 minutes or until heated through, stirring often. Remove the cinnamon stick, cloves and lemon slices before serving.

Bourbon Slush

SERVES 20

1 tea bag
2 cups boiling water
1 (12-ounce) can frozen lemonade concentrate, thawed
1 (12-ounce) can frozen orange juice concentrate, thawed
2/3 cup sugar
6 cups water
1 to 2 cups bourbon

Steep the tea bag in 2 cups boiling water for 5 minutes. Discard the tea bag. Combine the tea, lemonade concentrate, orange juice concentrate, sugar, 6 cups water and the bourbon in a large freezer container and mix well. Freeze until solid or ready to serve. Thaw slightly and spoon into a punch bowl.

Champagne Punch

Serves 40

Ice Ring for Punch

Make an ice ring for punch using fruit juices instead of water. Make the ring in layers, allowing each to freeze before adding the next, with decorative fruits in the center. For a Bloody Mary punch bowl, use lemon, lime or tomato juice with lemon and lime slices or baby vegetables.

8 cups cranberry juice
1 (6-ounce) can frozen orange juice concentrate, thawed
1 (6-ounce) can frozen pineapple juice concentrate, thawed
1 (6-ounce) can frozen lemonade concentrate, thawed
1 cup brandy
2 bottles Champagne, chilled
Lemon and lime slices

Mix the cranberry juice, orange juice concentrate, pineapple juice concentrate, lemonade concentrate and brandy in a large punch bowl. Stir in the Champagne gently. Garnish with lemon and lime slices and serve immediately.

Limoncello

MAKES 7 TO 8 CUPS

2 pounds lemons
4 cups 100-proof vodka
3 cups sugar
3 cups water

Rinse the lemons well in warm water. Remove the peel from the lemons. Place the peels in a glass pitcher, discarding the lemons. Add the vodka. Marinate, covered, at room temperature for 1 week. Combine the sugar and water in a saucepan and heat over medium-high heat until the sugar has dissolved, stirring occasionally. Add to the vodka mixture and mix well. Strain into bottles, discarding the peels. Chill for 1 month before serving.

Limoncello Martini

MAKES VARIABLE AMOUNT

1 part limoncello
1 part pomegranate juice
2 parts vodka
Pomegranate seeds

Combine the limoncello, pomegranate juice and vodka in a cocktail shaker and add ice to fill. Shake until chilled and strain into martini glasses. Float pomegranate seeds on top.

A STAR FELL ON ALABAMA

Early Alabama maps described the Wetumpka area as "structurally disturbed." That was the common wisdom until Alabama geologist Tony Neathery made a startling observation in 1972. The earth in the hills is turned upside down. We now know that this geological bowl is actually a meteor crater formed 80 million years ago when a star literally fell on Alabama. Geologists today estimate that the meteor was 1,000 feet in diameter and would completely fill a structure the size of Auburn University's Jordan-Hare Stadium.

The crater is often compared to a giant tossed salad in which ancient layers of rock are tossed with newer rocks and soil. The bowl is about five miles across and is considered to be the best-preserved marine impact crater on earth. The western crater remnants jut out of the Coosa near downtown Wetumpka, creating the rapids that gave the city its name, which is Creek for "rumbling waters."

The impact also altered the water table, creating many springs within the crater. In the early 1800s one spring, Harrowgate, became the center of social life in Wetumpka. Harrowgate Springs was the site of a large hotel where many famous guests were hosted. A favorite servant at the hotel was a young slave girl with a memorable name. She died as a child and men who were frequent guests of the hotel erected a tombstone in her memory inscribed:

> *Henry Ritter, Ema Ritter, Dema Ritter*
> *Sweet Potatoe, Creamatarter*
> *Caroline Bostick*
> *Daughter of Bob and Suckey Catlen*
> *Born at Social Circle Georgia in 1843*
> *Died in Wetumpka in 1852*

The meteor left an indelible impact on the geography of our area, creating scenic hills and valleys for business locations, church sites, and residential areas where our own "crater Episcopalians" live.

This section was generously sponsored by

THE WETUMPKA HERALD

Soups and Salads

WORRIES GO

DOWN BETTER

WITH SOUP.

JEWISH PROVERB

Patsy Riley's Vegetable Soup

SERVES 8 TO 10

Alabama's First Lady, Patsy Riley, is an accomplished and exuberant hostess. Her parties are legendary, but her heart is in the cooking she does for her family. This recipe is one she defines as "home."

1 pound beef tips
1 teaspoon salt
1 teaspoon minced garlic
1/4 to 1/2 head cabbage, thinly sliced, or 1 (10-ounce) package angel hair coleslaw mix
1 (16-ounce) can stewed tomatoes
1 (16-ounce) can tomato sauce
1 (10-ounce) can beef consommé
1 (14-ounce) can green beans, peas or butter beans
1 (15-ounce) can whole kernel corn
3 or 4 potatoes, peeled and cut into cubes
1 large onion, diced
3 carrots, sliced
3 ribs celery, sliced
1/2 cup (1 stick) butter, cut into pieces
2 tablespoons sugar
2 tablespoons Worcestershire sauce or Dale's seasoning sauce

Brown the beef tips in a stockpot or large heavy saucepan. Cover with water and bring to a simmer. Stir in the salt and garlic. Reduce the temperature and cook on low heat for 1 hour. Remove the beef and skim off any fat from the cooking liquid. Return the beef to the stockpot. Stir in the cabbage, tomatoes, tomato sauce, consommé, green beans, corn, potatoes, onion, carrots, celery, butter, sugar and Worcestershire sauce. Cook for 1 hour or until the vegetables are tender, stirring occasionally. (**NOTE:** *If your family likes things a bit spicy, add one or more 10-ounce cans of diced tomatoes with green chiles. You may use chicken pieces and chicken consommé instead of the beef tips and beef consommé. Remove the chicken from the bones and cut into cubes before returning to the liquid.)*

Sausage and Turnip Green Soup

SERVES 6

1 pound bulk pork sausage
1 onion, chopped
1 garlic clove, minced
2 (15-ounce) cans turnip greens
1 (15-ounce) can black-eyed peas
1 (15-ounce) can Great Northern beans, drained and rinsed
1 (15-ounce) can navy beans, drained and rinsed
1 (10-ounce) can diced tomatoes with green chiles
1 (14-ounce) can low-fat chicken broth
1 cup water

Combine the sausage, onion and garlic in a stockpot or large heavy saucepan and cook until the sausage is brown and cooked through. Drain well and return to the stockpot. Stir in the turnip greens, undrained black-eyed peas, Great Northern beans, navy beans, diced tomatoes with green chiles, chicken broth and water and bring to a simmer. Simmer for 15 minutes or until the soup is well blended, stirring occasionally. (**NOTE:** *This is a fast and filling soup especially great to serve in the wintertime.)*

New Year's Day Soup

SERVES 4 TO 6

A serving of this hearty soup should insure a happy new year for you and your family. Greens for money, peas for luck and ham hock for health are traditions we bank on.

1 small ham hock, cut into cubes
12 cups water
8 ounces Conecuh spicy and hot sausage or any spicy sausage, sliced
1 onion, chopped
1 bell pepper, chopped
1 tomato, chopped
1 garlic clove, crushed
1 bay leaf
3 (10-ounce) packages frozen collard greens
2 (15-ounce) cans black-eyed peas
3 potatoes, peeled and cut into cubes
1/2 teaspoon sugar or sugar substitute
Salt to taste

Boil the ham hock in the water in a stockpot or large heavy saucepan for 30 minutes or longer. Add the sausage, onion, bell pepper, tomato, garlic and bay leaf and simmer for 30 minutes. Add the collard greens, black-eyed peas, potatoes, sugar and salt and simmer for 20 minutes, adding more water as needed to cover. Serve with cornbread. (**NOTE:** *On any day but New Year's Day, you may substitute Great Northern beans for the black-eyed peas. We use Conecuh sausage, a favorite local sausage made in Evergreen, Alabama, but you may use your favorite local brand.)*

Our Place She Crab Soup

Serves 8

Our Place is a restaurant that would make any city proud. We are especially proud to have it in Wetumpka, beautifully located in a former filling station and garage. Owner and chef David Funderburk, along with his wife, Mona, shared their famous She Crab Soup recipe with us.

1 yellow onion, finely chopped
1 cup (2 sticks) butter, melted
1 cup all-purpose flour
4 cups heavy cream
1/2 cup Paul Prudhommes's Seafood Magic
8 cups milk
1 cup red wine
1 tablespoon salt, or to taste
2 tablespoons pepper
1 pound lump or claw crab meat

Sauté the onion in the butter in a 8-quart stockpot over low heat until transparent. Whisk in the flour and cook for 8 minutes, whisking constantly. Add the cream gradually, whisking constantly until well blended. Add the seafood seasoning. Cook for 5 to 10 minutes or until thickened, stirring often. Add the milk. Cook for 20 minutes or until thickened, stirring often. Add the wine, salt, pepper and crab meat and cook for 10 minutes, stirring often.

Oyster Artichoke Soup

SERVES 6

1 large onion, chopped
1 bunch green onions, chopped
1/2 cup (1 stick) butter, melted
2 garlic cloves, crushed or minced
2 tablespoons chopped parsley
2 (16-ounce) cans artichoke hearts, drained and cut into quarters
2 (10-ounce) cans cream of mushroom soup
1 cup oyster liquor or water
1 bay leaf
2 dozen (or more) shucked oysters
Salt and pepper to taste

Sauté the onions in the butter in a large heavy saucepan until transparent. Add the garlic and parsley and sauté for 2 to 3 minutes. Add the artichoke hearts and sauté for 3 to 4 minutes. Add the soup, oyster liquor and bay leaf. Cook for 20 minutes, stirring occasionally. Add the oysters and cook for 5 minutes. Simmer for up to 30 minutes to allow the flavors to meld. Discard the bay leaf.

Cream of Garlic Soup

SERVES 8

This recipe originated at Bayona Restaurant in New Orleans.

2 pounds onions, coarsely chopped
2 cups chopped garlic cloves
2 tablespoons olive oil
2 tablespoons butter, melted
6 cups (or more) chicken broth
1 bouquet garni
2 cups (1/2-inch) dry French bread pieces
1 cup half-and-half
Salt and pepper to taste

Sauté the onions and garlic in the hot olive oil and butter in a 4-quart heavy stockpot for 30 minutes or until deep golden brown. Add the chicken broth and bouquet garni and bring to a boil. Stir in the bread and simmer for 10 minutes or until the bread is soft. Remove the bouquet garni and discard. Process the soup in a blender until smooth. Strain through a medium mesh strainer back into the stockpot. Heat through, whisking in more chicken broth as needed to reach the desired consistency. Stir in the half-and-half. Season with salt and pepper. (**NOTE:** *Make a bouquet garni by tying parsley stems, thyme sprigs and a bay leaf together with kitchen twine.)*

Pumpkin Chowder

SERVES 8

This recipe originated at the Georgia Grille in Atlanta, Georgia.

1 cup chopped onion
1 tablespoon chopped jalapeño chile, puréed
2 tablespoons vegetable oil
3 cups chopped potatoes
6 cups chicken stock
2 to 4 cups puréed pumpkin
1 cup heavy cream
1/4 cup chopped hickory-smoked poblano chiles (see note below)
1 teaspoon cumin
1 teaspoon salt

Sauté the onion and jalapeño chile in the hot oil in a large stockpot until the onion is translucent. Add the potatoes and sauté for 1 minute. Add the chicken stock and bring to a boil. Cook until the potatoes are tender. Remove approximately 2 cups of the potatoes and place them in a food process or blender. Process until smooth. Reduce the heat and return the puréed potatoes to the stockpot. Add the pumpkin and cream and stir until combined. Bring to a simmer and stir in the poblano chiles, cumin and salt. (**NOTE:** *Smoke the pobano chiles on a grill rack over a hickory smoke fire or arrange the poblano chiles with lit presoaked hickory chips in a covered fireproof container until the fire burns out.)*

Roasted Red Bell Pepper Soup

SERVES 4 TO 6

4 large red bell peppers, roasted, peeled and seeded
2 (28-ounce) cans stewed tomatoes, drained
2 garlic cloves, minced
3 tablespoons extra-virgin olive oil
3 cups chicken stock
Salt and pepper to taste
1/2 cup white wine
1/2 teaspoon dill weed

Process the bell peppers and tomatoes in a food processor until puréed, leaving some chunks. Sauté the garlic in the hot olive oil; do not brown. Stir in the bell pepper mixture and chicken stock and bring to a boil. Season with salt and pepper. Stir in the wine and dill weed and simmer for 10 minutes. Serve hot or cold.

Tomato, Lemon and Carrot Soup

Serves 10

2 onions, chopped
3 tablespoons sunflower oil
2 tablespoons butter, melted
1 pound carrots, peeled and chopped
4 cups chicken stock
1 (15-ounce) can tomatoes
Grated zest of 2 lemons
Juice of 1 lemon
Yogurt
Grated carrot, lemon slices or
finely chopped parsley

Sauté the onions in the hot sunflower oil and butter for 5 minutes. Add the carrots and sauté for 2 minutes. Stir in the chicken stock, tomatoes and lemon zest and bring to a simmer. Simmer, partially covered, for 30 minutes or until the carrots are tender. Let stand until cool. Process the soup in a food processor or with an immersion blender until smooth. Strain the soup through a mesh strainer into a clean saucepan. Stir in the lemon juice. Cook until heated through. Spoon into soup bowls and top with a dollop of yogurt. Garnish with grated carrot, a lemon slice or finely chopped parsley.

Tarragon Tomato Soup

SERVES 4 TO 6

1 large onion, sliced
1 tablespoon olive oil
2 pounds tomatoes
4 cups chicken stock
1 tablespoon tomato paste
1 tablespoon crushed tarragon
1 teaspoon thyme
1 bay leaf
Dash of Tabasco sauce
Salt and pepper to taste

Sauté the onion in the hot olive oil in a large heavy saucepan until tender. Peel and core the tomatoes and cut into quarters. Add to the onion mixture. Stir in the chicken stock, tomato paste, tarragon, thyme, bay leaf and Tabasco sauce. Season with salt and pepper. Simmer for 30 minutes. Press through a mesh strainer or process through a food mill into a clean saucepan. Adjust seasoning if needed and serve hot or cold.

Wetumpka has the distinction of being located approximately equidistant from Flea Hop and Slap Out.

Spring Minestrone

SERVES 6

Alabama's most renowned chef, Frank Stitt, of Highlands Bar and Grill, Chez FonFon, and Bottega Restaurant and Café, generously shared this recipe.

Soup

2 onions, cut into quarters and thinly sliced
4 bulb onions, thinly sliced
4 carrots, peeled and cut into 1/2-inch pieces
2 leeks, thinly sliced
1 garlic clove, minced
2 tablespoons olive oil
1 tablespoon butter, melted
5 cups vegetable broth, water or chicken stock
10 small new potatoes, cut into 1/2-inch cubes
8 ounces small button mushrooms, cut into quarters
1/2 cup fava beans, peeled (optional)
1 cup sliced asparagus
1 cup sweet peas
4 small zucchini, cut into 1/2-inch cubes
1/2 cup chopped fresh mint, basil or parsley
Extra-virgin olive oil for drizzling
Freshly grated Parmigiano-Reggiano

Lemon Pesto

1/2 cup chopped fresh mint, basil or parsley
1/4 garlic clove
Lemon zest
Salt to taste
1/4 cup extra virgin olive oil

To prepare the soup, sauté the onions, carrots, leeks and garlic in 2 tablespoons hot olive oil and the butter in a large heavy stockpot over medium-low heat for 10 minutes or until tender. Stir in the broth, potatoes, mushrooms and fava beans and simmer for 10 minutes. Add the asparagus, peas and zucchini and simmer for 5 minutes. Serve the soup in warm bowls. Garnish with a large pinch of the chopped mint, a drizzle of olive oil, a sprinkle of cheese or a dollop of lemon pesto.

To prepare the lemon pesto, crush the mint, garlic, lemon zest and salt with a pestle in a mortar. Add the olive oil gradually, mixing constantly until incorporated.

Gazpacho

SERVES 15

This recipe is a favorite at Glen Ella Springs in the North Georgia mountains.

1 (46-ounce) can vegetable juice cocktail
3/4 cup (1/8-inch dice) green bell pepper
3/4 cup (1/8-inch dice) celery
3/4 cup (1/8-inch dice) cucumber
1/3 cup (1/8-inch dice) onion
1/3 cup red wine vinegar
1/4 cup olive oil
3 tablespoons sugar
2 tablespoons Worcestershire sauce
1 1/2 teaspoons salt
1 teaspoon minced garlic (about 1 clove)
1/2 teaspoon pepper
1/2 teaspoon Tabasco sauce
1 cup sour cream
1 tablespoon horseradish, or to taste

Combine the vegetable juice cocktail, bell pepper, celery, cucumber and onion in a large bowl and mix well. Stir in the red wine vinegar, olive oil, sugar, Worcestershire sauce, salt, garlic, pepper and Tabasco sauce. Chill, covered, for 8 to 10 hours. Adjust seasonings as needed. Combine the sour cream and horseradish in a bowl and mix well. Serve the chilled gazpacho in soup bowls and garnish with a dollop of the horseradish sauce. (**NOTE:** *To prepare a Gazpacho Aspic, combine 3 envelopes unflavored gelatin with some of the soup liquid and let stand until softened. Stir the gelatin mixture into the soup. Divide the soup among aspic molds and chill, covered, for 8 to 10 hours or until firm. Serve with the horseradish sauce.)*

Artichoke and Rice Salad

SERVES 4 TO 6

1 (6-ounce) package long grain and wild rice mix
1 (14-ounce) can artichoke hearts, drained and chopped
12 pimento-stuffed olives, sliced
1 cup chopped celery
1/2 cup mayonnaise
3 green onions, chopped
1 (2-ounce) jar chopped pimento, drained
1 teaspoon curry powder

Cook the rice according to the package directions, omitting the butter if any is used. Let stand until cool. Combine the rice mixture, artichoke hearts, olives, celery, mayonnaise, green onions, pimento, and curry powder in a large bowl and mix until combined. (**NOTE:** *You may use yellow rice instead of the long grain and wild rice for a different taste and vibrant color.)*

Bread Salad

SERVES 6 TO 8

3 tablespoons torn fresh basil
1 tablespoon minced fresh parsley
2 teaspoons chopped fresh oregano
1/2 teaspoon salt
1/4 teaspoon pepper
2 large tomatoes, chopped
1/2 red onion, thinly sliced into rings
1/2 cup olive oil
3 tablespoons red wine vinegar
1 pound (one-day-old) Italian bread, cut into 1-inch cubes

Combine the basil, parsley, oregano, salt and pepper in a bowl and mix well. Combine the tomatoes, onion, olive oil, vinegar and half the basil mixture in a bowl and mix well. Let stand for 10 minutes. Arrange the bread evenly in an 8×8-inch baking dish. Pour the tomato mixture evenly over the bread. Sprinkle the remaining basil mixture on top.

Coleslaw with Tomatoes

SERVES 6 TO 8

1/3 cup mayonnaise
1 tablespoon apple cider vinegar
1 (10-ounce) package angel hair coleslaw mix
1 large tomato, peeled and chopped
1 large cucumber, peeled and thinly sliced
4 green onions, thinly sliced
Salt and pepper to taste

Combine the mayonnaise and vinegar in a large bowl and blend until smooth. Add the coleslaw mix, tomato, cucumber and green onions and toss until coated. Season with salt and a generous amount of black pepper. (**NOTE:** *The coleslaw can be kept in the refrigerator, covered, for 2 to 3 days; drain any liquid that accumulates before serving.)*

Greek Salad

SERVES 6 TO 8

1 envelope Italian salad dressing mix
2 pints cherry tomatoes, cut into halves
2 cucumbers, cut into quarters and sliced
1 red onion, chopped
1 green bell pepper, chopped
1 red, yellow or orange bell pepper, chopped
3/4 cup sliced green olives
3/4 cup sliced black olives
4 ounces Monterey Jack cheese, cut into small pieces
2 ounces feta cheese, crumbled

Prepare the salad dressing mix in a bowl according to the package directions, using red wine vinegar and olive oil. Combine the tomatoes, cucumber, onion, bell peppers, green olives, black olives, Monterey Jack cheese and feta cheese in a bowl. Pour the salad dressing on top and toss until well coated. Chill, covered, in the refrigerator for 3 to 4 hours.

Grapefruit Aspic Salad with Creamy Cucumber Dressing

SERVES 8

Grapefruit Aspic Salad
1 1/2 tablespoons unflavored gelatin
1 cup cold water
1 cup boiling water
3/4 cup sugar
3 tablespoons fresh lemon juice
3 large grapefruit
3/4 cup chopped celery
1/2 cup blanched slivered almonds

Creamy Cucumber Dressing
1 cucumber
1/2 cup heavy whipping cream
2 tablespoons fresh lemon juice
1/4 teaspoon salt
1/8 teaspoon paprika

To prepare the salad, combine the gelatin and cold water in a bowl and let stand until softened. Dissolve the gelatin mixture in the boiling water in a large heatproof bowl. Stir in the sugar and lemon juice. Chill, covered, until the gelatin mixture is almost set. Peel and segment the grapefruit, reserving the juice. Fold the grapefruit segments and reserved juice into the gelatin mixture. Fold in the celery and almonds. Spoon into a ring mold or individual molds and chill, covered, until firm. Invert onto a serving platter lined with lettuce leaves and remove the mold. Serve with mayonnaise or creamy cucumber dressing.

To prepare the dressing, peel and seed the cucumber. Grate or finely chop the cucumber and drain well. Whip the cream in a mixing bowl until stiff peaks form. Add the lemon juice, salt and paprika, beating constantly. Fold in the cucumber.

Tootsie's Potato Salad

Serves 8 to 10

3 pounds new potatoes
1/3 cup extra-virgin olive oil
1/3 cup red wine vinegar
1/4 cup stone-ground mustard
1/2 teaspoon salt
1/2 teaspoon freshly ground pepper
1 red onion, chopped
Chopped fresh parsley

Cook the potatoes in water to cover in a saucepan for 15 minutes or until tender; drain. Let stand until slightly cooled. Combine the olive oil, vinegar, stone-ground mustard, salt and pepper in a jar with a tight-fitting lid and seal tightly. Shake to mix. Pour over the potatoes and add the onions. Toss until coated and spoon into a serving bowl. Garnish with parsley.

After cooking the potatoes for potato salad and draining them, add a bit of chicken stock or vegetable stock (about 1/2 cup per 2 pounds cooked potatoes) and toss them lightly. Let stand for 20 minutes. This will allow them to absorb the stock instead of absorbing all of the oil in the mayonnaise, which will make the potatoes seem dry.

Wilted Spinach Salad

Serves 4 to 6

6 strips bacon
1/3 cup bottled French salad dressing or Grandmother's French Dressing (see below)
1 pound fresh spinach leaves
2 hard-cooked eggs, chopped
3 tablespoons chopped pimento

Cook the bacon in a skillet until very crisp. Drain, reserving the pan drippings. Crumble the bacon. Strain the reserved pan drippings into a large bowl. Add the salad dressing and blend until smooth. Immediately add the spinach and toss until coated and wilted. Divide among salad plates and top evenly with the bacon, eggs and pimento. Serve immediately.

Grandmother's French Dressing

Makes about 1 cup

This is a versatile old-fashioned vinaigrette.

2/3 cup vegetable oil
1/3 cup cider vinegar
1 1/4 teaspoons salt
1 1/2 teaspoons sugar
1 teaspoon Worcestershire sauce
1/2 teaspoon dry mustard
1/2 teaspoon paprika

Combine the oil, vinegar, salt, sugar, Worcestershire sauce, dry mustard and paprika in a jar with a tight-fitting lid and seal tightly. Shake to mix. (**Note:** *Add horseradish to taste for a change of pace.)*

Zippy Tomato Aspic

SERVES 7 TO 8

1 3/4 cups vegetable juice cocktail
1 (3-ounce) package raspberry-flavored gelatin
1/2 cup finely chopped celery
1/2 cup chopped pimento-stuffed olives
2 tablespoons horseradish
1 tablespoon lemon juice
1/2 teaspoon celery salt
1/2 teaspoon Worcestershire sauce
1/4 teaspoon salt
Lettuce leaves
Mayonnaise
Basil

Bring the vegetable juice cocktail to a boil in a saucepan. Stir in the gelatin until dissolved. Let stand until room temperature. Stir in the celery, olives, horseradish, lemon juice, celery salt, Worcestershire sauce and salt. Pour into seven individual molds or a baking pan. Chill, covered, until set. Invert onto a serving platter lined with lettuce leaves. Garnish with a dollop of mayonnaise and basil. (**NOTE:** *For a beautiful presentation, use a ring mold and fill the open center with chicken salad. You may add chopped vegetables such as green onions, green bell pepper and cucumbers. This can help stretch the recipe to fill eight individual molds.)*

Pasta Salad with Tomatoes and Peas

SERVES 10 TO 12

1 large garlic clove, minced
1/4 teaspoon salt
1/3 cup white wine vinegar
2 tablespoons water
2 teaspoons salt
1/2 teaspoon sugar
2 teaspoons minced fresh tarragon, or 1/2 teaspoon dried tarragon
Pepper to taste
1/2 cup olive oil
16 ounces pasta shells
Salt to taste
8 ounces fresh or frozen peas, thawed (about 1 1/2 cups)
2 pints red or yellow pear tomatoes, cherry tomatoes or a combination, cut into halves
1/2 cup shredded fresh basil leaves

Mash the garlic and 1/4 teaspoon salt together until of a paste consistency. Combine the garlic mixture, vinegar, water, 2 teaspoons salt, the sugar, tarragon and pepper in a bowl and whisk until combined. Add the olive oil in a fine stream, whisking constantly until incorporated. Cook the pasta in boiling salted water in a large saucepan until al dente. Rinse and drain the pasta. Place the pasta in a large serving bowl. Add the vinaigrette, peas, tomatoes and basil. Toss until combined and well coated.

Poppy Seed Dressing

MAKES 3 1/2 CUPS

2 cups vegetable oil
1 1/2 cups sugar
2/3 cup vinegar
3 tablespoons poppy seeds
3 tablespoons onion juice or grated onion
2 teaspoons dry mustard
2 teaspoons salt

Process the oil, sugar, vinegar, poppy seeds, onion juice, dry mustard and salt in a food processor until combined. Serve over a fresh fruit salad or a spinach salad with strawberries, peaches, bananas or pears.

Strawberry Dressing

MAKES 3 1/2 CUPS

1 (10-ounce) package frozen sliced strawberries, thawed slightly
2/3 cup mayonnaise
1 cup strawberry yogurt

Combine the strawberries and mayonnaise in a bowl and mix well. Fold in the yogurt. Chill, covered, for at least 1 hour. Serve over honeydew wedges and fresh strawberries cut into halves, or as a dip for fresh fruit.

Herb Vinaigrette

MAKES 1/2 CUP

1/4 cup olive oil
2 tablespoons wine vinegar or balsamic vinegar
1 teaspoon chopped parsley
1 teaspoon chopped chives
1 teaspoon chopped onion
1 teaspoon salt
1/4 teaspoon pepper
Minced garlic to taste

Combine the olive oil, vinegar, parsley, chives, onion, salt, pepper and garlic in a jar with a tight-fitting lid and seal tightly. Shake to mix. Let stand for 3 minutes or longer for flavors to meld. Serve on tossed salads.

THE GRITS ARE FREE

A love of grits must be woven into the DNA of Southerners as they are such an indispensable part of our cuisine, or maybe our devotion to them is the result of grits being the first solid food for many a Southern child. Nothing illustrates the essentialness of grits more than a situation which resulted in a court case in Montgomery County. A patron at a local restaurant had been served breakfast without grits, which were included on the menu with the breakfast he ordered. The man considered the grits to be necessary for his enjoyment of his breakfast. Therefore, when he went to the cash register to pay, he deducted $1.50 from the total as compensation for not being served grits. He and the restaurant owner proceeded to have a vociferous argument at the front counter.

The restaurant owner argued, "You cannot deduct any money from the total as the grits are free with the meal."

The man retaliated, "How can the grits be free?"

The argument turned personal, and the man left the restaurant in a huff without paying the $1.50 for the grits. The restaurant owner was so enraged that he filed suit against the patron.

The case ended up in the Montgomery County Circuit Court. As might be expected, anyone who worked in the courthouse and who could, went to the courtroom to observe the "grits" case. Not one of the observers can remember what the judge ruled in the case as they were trying so hard not to laugh, but they all vividly recall the plaintiff's constant refrain, "The grits are free."

Breakfast and Breads

GIVE US
THIS DAY
OUR DAILY
BREAD.

MATTHEW 6:11

Eggs Florentine Frittata

SERVES 8

9 eggs
2 cups low-fat cottage cheese
1 cup (4 ounces) shredded Cheddar cheese
1/2 cup feta cheese, crumbled
1/2 teaspoon nutmeg
1/2 teaspoon white pepper
1/2 teaspoon salt
2 (10-ounce) packages frozen chopped spinach, thawed and drained
1 red bell pepper, thinly sliced

Beat the eggs lightly in a bowl with a whisk. Add the cottage cheese, Cheddar cheese, feta cheese, nutmeg, white pepper and salt and mix well. Stir in the spinach. Pour into a 9×13-inch baking dish sprayed with nonstick cooking spray. Arrange the bell pepper on top. Bake at 375 degrees for 45 minutes or until the eggs are set. Cool slightly before serving. (**NOTE:** *You may make this dish in advance and refrigerate. Reheat in the oven when ready to serve.)*

Eggs "Bama"-dict

Serves 12

Eggs

6 English muffins, split into halves
Butter to taste
12 slices Canadian bacon
15 eggs
1 cup (4 ounces) shredded sharp Cheddar cheese
Salt and pepper to taste

Hollandaise Sauce

4 egg yolks
1 tablespoon lemon juice
1/2 teaspoon salt
Dash of Tabasco sauce
1/2 cup (1 stick) butter

To prepare the eggs, toast the English muffin halves and spread with butter. Brown the Canadian bacon in a skillet; drain. Whisk the eggs in a bowl until light and frothy. Add the cheese, salt and pepper and mix well. Arrange the muffin halves in the bottom of a baking dish, split side up. Top each muffin half with a slice of Canadian bacon. Pour the egg mixture evenly over the Canadian bacon. Bake at 350 degrees for 20 to 25 minutes or until the eggs are set. Let stand for 5 minutes before serving. Slice into squares around the muffin halves.

To prepare the sauce, combine the egg yolks, lemon juice, salt and Tabasco sauce in a blender and process until smooth. Bring the butter to a simmer in a saucepan. Remove from the heat and immediately add to the egg yolk mixture in a fine stream, processing constantly at high spend until combined.

To serve, top each serving with a spoonful of Hollandaise sauce. (**Note:** *The Hollandaise Sauce can be kept warm in a baking dish placed in a pan of hot water.)*

Basic Brunch Quiche

Serves 12

1 bunch asparagus
8 ounces fresh mushrooms, sliced
1 onion, finely chopped
Melted butter or olive oil for sautéing
6 eggs, lightly beaten
2 cups cottage cheese
1 cup (scant) biscuit mix
1 cup milk
1 cup (4 ounces) shredded sharp Cheddar cheese
1/4 cup (1/2 stick) butter, melted
Salt and pepper to taste

Place the asparagus in a microwave-safe dish. Microwave on High for 2 minutes. Drain and pat dry. Let stand until cool and then cut on the diagonal into 1-inch pieces. Sauté the mushrooms and onion in butter in a skillet until tender. Drain and let stand until cool. Combine the eggs, cottage cheese, biscuit mix, milk, Cheddar cheese and butter and mix well. Stir in the mushroom mixture and asparagus. Pour into a greased 9×13-inch baking dish. Bake at 350 degrees for 45 minutes or until set. Let stand for 10 minutes before slicing. (**Note:** *You may use any combination of vegetables and meats. Try using ham, shrimp, peppers and/or mushrooms with cheese.)*

Potato-Crusted Sausage Quiche

SERVES 6

8 ounces bulk pork sausage
2 cups egg substitute, or 8 eggs
1 cup cottage cheese
2 tablespoons all-purpose flour
1/2 teaspoon garlic salt
1/2 teaspoon Tabasco sauce
1/4 teaspoon pepper
1 cup (4 ounces) shredded Cheddar cheese
1/2 green bell pepper, chopped
2 scallions, chopped
Chopped mushrooms to taste
4 to 6 potatoes

Cook the sausage in a skillet until cooked through and crumbly. Drain and let stand until cool. Combine the egg substitute, cottage cheese, flour, garlic salt, Tabasco sauce and pepper in a large bowl and mix well. Stir in the sausage, cheese, bell pepper, scallions and mushrooms. Peel and slice the potatoes 1/4 inch thick. Arrange the potato slices in a single layer over the bottom and up the side of a 10-inch pie plate sprayed with nonstick cooking spray. Pour the egg mixture into the potato-lined pie plate. Bake at 375 degrees for 45 minutes or until a knife inserted in the center comes out clean. Let stand for 5 minutes before slicing. (**NOTE:** *You may use 8 ounces chopped deli ham instead of the sausage.)*

In Titus, home of Joe Sewell of the Baseball Hall of Fame, in the 1940s an egg boiling happened regularly on the Saturday night before Easter. Residents came to the community center with their eggs and gathered around a black iron wash pot heated by a mighty fire. Eggs were dumped into the boiling pot and contests ensued. Who could eat their eggs the least cooked, and who could eat the most?

Cheesy Sausage Muffins

MAKES 1 DOZEN

4 ounces bulk pork sausage
1 cup biscuit mix
1/2 cup (2 ounces) shredded Cheddar cheese
3 ounces cream cheese, cut into small cubes
1/4 cup chopped green onions (optional)
2/3 cup milk
2 eggs, lightly beaten

Cook the sausage in a skillet until cooked through and crumbly; drain. Combine the sausage, biscuit mix, Cheddar cheese, cream cheese and green onions in a bowl and mix well. Combine the milk and eggs in a bowl and blend until smooth. Add to the sausage mixture and mix until combined. Spoon into greased muffin cups, filling two-thirds full. Bake at 350 degrees for 16 to 18 minutes.

Sausage Egg Soufflé

SERVES 6

1 pound bulk pork sausage
6 slices bread, toasted
6 eggs
2 cups milk
1/2 teaspoon dry mustard
Salt and pepper to taste
1 cup (4 ounces) shredded Cheddar cheese

Cook the sausage in a skillet until cooked through and crumbly; drain. Slice the toast into quarters. Whisk the eggs, milk and dry mustard in a bowl until combined. Season with salt and pepper. Layer the toast, sausage and cheese one-half at a time in six large ramekins or one large baking dish sprayed with nonstick cooking spray. Pour the egg mixture over the top. Bake at 325 degrees for 45 to 60 minutes or until set. Let stand for 5 minutes before serving. (**NOTE:** *This soufflé can be made 24 hours in advance and reheated when ready to serve.)*

Zesty Grits Casserole

SERVES 8

1 pound Polish sausage, sliced
1 cup quick-cooking grits
1 1/2 cups (6 ounces) shredded sharp Cheddar cheese
1/2 cup (1 stick) butter
1 (10-ounce) can diced tomatoes with green chiles
1 egg
1 teaspoon salt, or to taste

Sauté the sausage in a skillet until light brown; drain. Cook the grits using the package directions. Stir in the cheese, butter, tomatoes with green chiles, egg and salt. Add the sausage and mix well. Spoon into a baking dish. Bake at 350 degrees for 35 to 40 minutes or until heated through. (**NOTE:** *This recipe is great for Sunday brunch. This casserole can be made in advance and reheated when ready to serve.)*

Shrimp and Grits

SERVES 6

2 (14-ounce) cans chicken broth
2 cups half-and-half
1/4 teaspoon salt
1 1/4 cups grits
2 eggs
1 cup (4 ounces) shredded sharp Cheddar cheese
2 tablespoons butter
1 large yellow bell pepper, chopped or sliced
1 red bell pepper, chopped or sliced
2 tablespoons olive oil
1 1/2 pounds small or medium shrimp, peeled
Salt and pepper to taste
Chopped green onions, crumbled crisp-cooked bacon or cooked sausage (optional)

Bring the broth, half-and-half and 1/4 teaspoon salt to a simmer in a heavy saucepan. Add the grits gradually, stirring constantly until combined. Cook according to the package directions. Beat the eggs in a mixing bowl until light and frothy. Add the grits gradually, beating constantly until combined. Stir in the cheese and butter and mix well. Spoon into a 3-quart baking dish sprayed with nonstick cooking spray.

Sauté the bell peppers in the hot olive oil in a skillet until tender. Remove the skillet from the heat and add the shrimp, tossing until coated. Season with salt and pepper to taste. Spoon on top of the grits mixture. Bake at 325 degrees for 30 to 40 minutes or until heated through. Garnish with green onions, bacon or sausage. (**NOTE:** *Covered and placed in an insulated cooler or a warmer, this dish will keep warm for 2 1/2 to 3 hours.)*

Hissy Fit Grits 'n' Greens Casserole

SERVES 8 TO 10

When author Mary Kay Andrews' book Hissy Fit *was first released, we tried her heroine's favorite recipe. It quickly became a local favorite.*

6 cups chicken broth
2 cups whipping cream or half-and-half
2 cups grits (not instant or quick-cooking)
Milk as needed
1 (16-ounce) package frozen collard greens, thawed
2 cups chicken broth
2 1/2 cups (10 ounces) grated Parmesan cheese
1 cup (2 sticks) butter
1/2 teaspoon freshly ground pepper
1 cup crumbled crisp-cooked bacon
Grated Parmesan cheese

Bring 6 cups chicken broth and the cream to a boil in a heavy saucepan. Add the grits gradually, stirring constantly until combined. Return to a boil and cover with a lid. Reduce the temperature to a simmer and cook for 25 to 30 minutes or until thick and creamy, stirring frequently. Add milk if needed to reach a proper grits consistency. (If you are a Southerner you know what that is. If you don't know, think slightly runny oatmeal.) Cook the collard greens in 2 cups chicken broth in a saucepan for 10 minutes or until tender. Drain in a colander, squeezing any excess liquid from the collard greens. Add 2 1/2 cups cheese, the butter and pepper to the cooked grits, stirring until the butter melts. Stir in the collard greens. Spoon into a greased baking dish. Sprinkle the bacon and additional cheese on top. Serve at room temperature or bake at 350 degrees until the top is golden brown.

Baked French Toast

SERVES 8

1 (12-ounce) French bread loaf, cut into 1/2-inch slices
1 cup packed brown sugar
1/2 cup (1 stick) butter, melted
1 teaspoon cinnamon
6 eggs
2 cups milk
Maple syrup

Arrange half the bread in a single layer in a greased 9×13-inch baking dish. Combine the brown sugar, butter and cinnamon in a bowl and mix well. Spread over the bread layer and top with the remaining bread. Combine the eggs and milk in a bowl and whisk until light and frothy. Pour evenly over the bread. Cover with aluminum foil and chill for 8 to 10 hours. Let stand at room temperature for 30 minutes. Bake, covered with the aluminum foil, at 350 degrees for 20 to 25 minutes. Uncover and bake for an additional 10 to 15 minutes or until cooked through and set. Drizzle with maple syrup and broil until brown and the syrup is bubbly.

Garlic Cheese Biscuits

MAKES 1 DOZEN

2 cups biscuit mix
2/3 cup milk
1/4 cup (1 ounce) shredded Cheddar cheese
1/4 cup (1/2 stick) butter, melted
1/2 teaspoon garlic powder

Combine the biscuit mix, milk and cheese in a bowl and mix well. Drop by spoonfuls onto an ungreased baking sheet. Bake at 350 degrees for 8 to 10 minutes or until cooked through and golden brown. Combine the butter and garlic powder in a small bowl and mix well. Brush the biscuits with the garlic butter before removing from the baking sheet. Serve hot. (**NOTE:** *For cheesier biscuits, double the amount of Cheddar cheese used.)*

Country Ham Sour Cream Biscuits

MAKES 4 DOZEN

2 to 4 slices country ham
1 cup (2 sticks) unsalted butter, softened
2 cups self-rising flour
1 cup sour cream

Cook the ham in a skillet until brown; drain. Let stand until cool and chop into cubes. Combine the butter, flour and sour cream in a bowl and blend until smooth. Drop by spoonfuls into miniature muffin cups. Press some of the ham into the center of each muffin cup. Bake at 350 degrees for 35 minutes or until golden brown. (**NOTE:** *These biscuits may be frozen and reheated when ready to serve.)*

Six-Week Bran Muffins

Makes 4 dozen

1 (15-ounce) package bran cereal with raisins
2 cups all-purpose flour
1 1/3 cups whole wheat flour
1 cup wheat germ
5 teaspoons baking soda
2 teaspoons salt
3/4 cup honey, or 3 cups sugar
4 eggs, lightly beaten
1 cup vegetable oil
4 cups buttermilk

Mix the cereal, all-purpose flour, whole wheat flour, wheat germ, baking soda and salt in a large bowl. Add the honey, eggs, oil and buttermilk and mix until combined. Spoon the batter into greased muffin cups, filling two-thirds full. Bake at 400 degrees for 15 to 20 minutes or until the muffins test done. Cover and store any unused batter in the refrigerator for up to 6 weeks.

Sweet Potato Muffins

Makes 2 dozen

1 1/2 cups all-purpose flour
2 tablespoons baking powder
1 teaspoon cinnamon
1/4 teaspoon nutmeg
1/4 teaspoon salt
1 1/4 cups sugar
1/2 cup (1 stick) butter, softened
1 1/4 cups mashed canned or cooked fresh sweet potatoes
2 eggs
1 cup milk
1/2 cup raisins, chopped
1/4 cup pecans, chopped
Cinnamon

Sift the flour, baking powder, cinnamon, nutmeg and salt together. Beat the sugar and butter in a mixing bowl until light and fluffy. Add the sweet potatoes and beat until smooth. Add the eggs and beat until combined. Add the sifted ingredients alternately with the milk, mixing well after each addition. Do not overmix. Fold in the raisins and pecans. Spoon the batter into greased muffin cups. Sprinkle with a small amount of cinnamon. Bake at 400 degrees for 25 minutes or until the muffins test done.

Crawfish Bread

SERVES 4 TO 6

1 loaf French bread or similar style bread
Sliced mozzarella cheese
Sliced Velveeta cheese
1 pound crawfish tails, peeled
1 bunch green onions, chopped
1/3 jar Paul Prudhomme's Seafood Magic
1/2 cup (1 stick) butter, melted

Slice the bread horizontally down the center and arrange on a baking sheet lined with heavy-duty aluminum foil. Arrange the mozzarella cheese down one-half of the bread and the Velveeta cheese down the other half. Sauté the crawfish, green onions and Seafood Magic in the butter in a skillet until the green onions are tender and the crawfish are cooked through and pink. Spoon the mixture over half the bread. Place the other half, cheese side down, on the crawfish mixture. Wrap the stuffed loaf together with the foil, sealing the ends well. Bake at 375 degrees for 30 minutes or until heated through. Slice and serve immediately.

Italian Pull-Apart Bread

SERVES 10 TO 15

2 (10-count) cans refrigerator buttermilk biscuits
1/2 cup (1 stick) butter, melted
1 envelope Italian salad dressing mix

Separate the biscuit dough. Cut each biscuit into quarters. Combine the butter and salad dressing mix in a bowl and mix well. Dip the biscuit pieces into the butter mixture and layer them in a bundt pan sprayed with nonstick cooking spray. Pour any remaining butter mixture over the top of the biscuits. Bake at 350 degrees for 15 to 30 minutes or until golden brown. Remove from the oven and immediately invert the pan onto a heatproof plate, leaving the pan over the bread for 5 minutes before removing. Serve warm. (**NOTE:** *The leftovers of this bread make great croutons for salads.)*

Tidewater Spoon Bread

SERVES 10

8 slices bacon
4 egg whites, at room temperature
1 1/2 cups water
3/4 cup cornmeal
1/4 cup (1/2 stick) unsalted butter, softened
2 cups (8 ounces) shredded Cheddar cheese
1 1/2 cups cooked corn kernels
2 garlic cloves, finely chopped
1/2 teaspoon salt
1 cup milk
4 egg yolks, lightly beaten

Cook the bacon in a skillet until crisp; drain and crumble. Beat the egg whites in a mixing bowl until stiff peaks form. Combine the water, cornmeal and butter in a saucepan and bring to a boil. Cook until thickened, stirring often. Remove from the heat and stir in the cheese, corn, garlic and salt. Add the milk, egg yolks and crumbled bacon and mix well. Fold in the egg whites. Spoon into a 1 1/2-quart baking dish sprayed with nonstick cooking spray. Bake at 325 degrees for 1 hour or until the middle is set. Serve hot.

Rosemary Raisin Walnut Bread

MAKES 2 LARGE LOAVES OR 4 SMALL LOAVES

3 cups milk
3 cups golden raisins
2 cups sugar
6 tablespoons unsalted butter, softened
3 eggs
1 teaspoon vanilla extract
4 1/2 cups unbleached flour
2 cups coarsely chopped walnuts
2 tablespoons double-acting baking powder
2 tablespoons chopped fresh rosemary leaves, or 2 teaspoons dried rosemary
2 teaspoons salt

Scald the milk in a small saucepan. Remove from the heat and stir in the raisins. Cover with a lid and let stand for 30 minutes or until lukewarm. Cream the sugar and butter in mixing bowl until light and fluffy. Add the raisin mixture, eggs and vanilla and mix well. Combine the flour, walnuts, baking powder, rosemary and salt in a bowl and mix well. Add to the raisin mixture and mix just until combined. Spoon the batter into two greased 4×8-inch loaf pans or four greased 3×5-inch loaf pans. Bake at 350 degrees for 1 hour and 15 minutes for the large loaves or 35 to 40 minutes for the small loaves, or until brown. Cool in the baking pans for 10 minutes. Remove to a wire rack to cool completely. (**NOTE:** *You may also use six greased 15-ounce cans, filling more than half full with batter and baking for 25 to 30 minutes or until brown.)*

Mexican Corn Bread

SERVES 6 TO 8

> *"You've got to continue to grow, or you're just like last night's corn bread—stale and dry."*
> —Loretta Lynn

1 pound bacon
1 1/2 cups all-purpose or self-rising yellow cornmeal
1 cup buttermilk
3 eggs, beaten
1 (14-ounce) can cream-style corn
1 (4-ounce) can chopped green chiles, or to taste
1 1/2 cups (6 ounces) shredded Cheddar cheese

Cook the bacon in a cast-iron skillet until crisp. Drain on paper towels, reserving the pan drippings in the skillet. Crumble the bacon. Place the skillet with the pan drippings in the oven and heat to 400 degrees. Combine the bacon, cornmeal, buttermilk, eggs, corn and green chiles in a bowl and mix well. Remove the skillet from the oven and carefully pour the pan drippings into the batter; mix well. The batter may sizzle. Pour half the batter into the skillet and sprinkle with the cheese. Pour the remaining batter on top. Bake until the top is brown. Let stand until cool before slicing.

Cracklin' Corn Bread

SERVES 8

1 1/2 cups buttermilk corn bread mix
1/4 cup flour
1 egg
1 teaspoon water
3 tablespoons bacon drippings
1 1/2 cups buttermilk
1 1/2 cups pork cracklings

Mix the corn bread mix and flour in a bowl. Combine the egg and water in a small bowl and beat until light and frothy. Add the egg mixture and bacon drippings to the dry ingredients and mix until the lumps are very small. Add the buttermilk and mix well. Stir in the pork cracklings. Spoon into a hot greased 9-inch cast-iron skillet and smooth the surface with the back of the spoon. Bake at 425 degrees for 30 to 40 minutes or until dark brown. Cut into eight wedges.

Wetu Hushpuppies

MAKES 50

3 cups cornmeal
2 cups (about) buttermilk
1 1/2 cups all-purpose flour
2 eggs
3 tablespoons sugar
1 tablespoon baking powder
1 or 2 onions, finely chopped
1 bell pepper, finely chopped
Vegetable oil for frying

Combine the cornmeal, buttermilk, flour, eggs, sugar and baking powder in a bowl and blend until smooth. Stir in the onion and bell pepper. Drop by teaspoonfuls into hot vegetable oil in a deep skillet or deep fryer in batches and fry until brown. Remove with a slotted spoon and drain on paper towels. Keep the hushpuppies warm until all have been made and are ready to be served.

Refrigerator French Bread

MAKES 2 LOAVES

If you need dough to rise and the house is too cool, turn your oven on for 60 seconds or long enough to reach 70 to 80 degrees. This is the perfect temperature for rising dough.

2 tablespoons butter
2 1/4 cups water
3 cups all-purpose flour
2 envelopes dry yeast
1 tablespoon sugar
1 tablespoon salt
3 1/4 to 3 3/4 cups all-purpose flour
Vegetable oil
1 egg white
1 tablespoon water

Melt the butter in a saucepan and stir in the water. Heat to 120 degrees. Combine 3 cups flour, the yeast, sugar and salt in a large mixing bowl. Add the butter mixture and mix at the highest speed for 3 minutes. Add 3 1/4 cups flour and knead for 3 minutes. Knead in additional flour if needed to make a soft dough. Place the dough in a greased bowl, turning to coat the surface. Let rise, covered, in a warm place for 30 minutes or doubled in bulk. Punch down the dough. Divide the dough into two portions. Roll each into a 8×15-inch rectangle. Roll as for a jelly roll, sealing the edge and the ends. Place seam side down on a greased baking sheet. Make shallow diagonal cuts on the top and brush with oil. Chill, covered, in the refrigerator for 2 to 24 hours. Remove from the refrigerator and let stand for 10 minutes before baking. Combine the egg white and water in a bowl and mix well. Brush the loaves with the egg wash. Bake at 400 degrees for 35 to 40 minutes or until golden brown. Remove to a wire rack to cool completely.

Refrigerator Rolls

MAKES 60

2 envelopes dry yeast
1/2 cup warm water
Pinch of sugar
1 cup shortening or butter
3/4 cup sugar
2 teaspoons salt
1 1/2 cups boiling water
6 to 7 cups all-purpose flour, or more as needed
1 egg, lightly beaten
Melted butter

Dissolve the yeast in 1/2 cup warm water in a small bowl and stir in a pinch of sugar. Combine the shortening, 3/4 cup sugar and the salt in a large bowl. Add 1 1/2 cups boiling water and stir until smooth. Let stand until lukewarm. Stir in the yeast mixture, flour and egg. Stir in additional flour if the dough is sticky. Chill, covered, in the refrigerator for 8 to 10 hours. Roll out the dough and cut with a biscuit cutter. Fold the circles in half. Dip each roll in melted butter or brush butter over the rolls. Place on a greased baking sheet and let rise for 2 hours or until doubled in bulk. Bake at 400 degrees for 12 to 15 minutes or until golden brown. (**NOTE:** *These rolls are delicious and keep for at least a week. This recipe may be doubled.)*

Adding a pinch of sugar to the yeast and warm water mixture will quicken the rising process.

BRIDGES TO KITH AND KIN

The bridges across the Coosa have joined east and west Wetumpka and provided the links that made the gatherings of friends and family possible. The first two bridges were short lived, but in 1844 Horace King, a freed slave and mechanic of great skill, designed a picturesque covered bridge to span the river. Three lanterns were lit at dusk, casting spooky shadows along the span, making the walk across the bridge at night distressing for adults but delightful for young people.

Tolls were collected for pedestrians, wagons, carriages, horse and rider, and even livestock. The toll was waived for anyone going to church. The tolls provided for the salary of the bridge keeper who collected an extra 25 cents toll if he had to open the gates late at night.

A Confederate veteran was known for tearing around the county on horseback, often at breakneck speeds. As he clattered across the bridge late one night, he tossed the tollkeeper 50 cents. The tollkeeper yelled, "Hold up there, Cap'n, I owe you change." The man galloped away, shouting over his shoulder, "I gotta come back, ain't I?"

When the landmark bridge was washed away in the great flood of 1886, an iron bridge was built. It deteriorated quickly.

As plans proceeded to replace the bridge, Probate Judge G. H. Howard stood firm for a concrete reinforced bridge. Fortunately for generations of travelers, Judge Howard prevailed and our distinctive and beautiful concrete suspension bridge was built. This bridge is the only one of its kind south of the Mason-Dixon Line and serves as the emblem for the City of Wetumpka. Visitors and life-long residents never fail to be delighted by the stunning design of the Bibb Graves Bridge.

This section was generously sponsored by

FIRST COMMUNITY BANK

Beef and Pork Main Dishes

ONE OF THE

NICEST THINGS ABOUT

LIFE IS THE WAY

WE MUST REGULARLY

STOP WHATEVER IT IS

WE ARE DOING

AND DEVOTE OUR ATTENTION

TO EATING.

LUCIANO
PAVAROTTI

Roasted Beef Tenderloin Glen Ella

SERVES 8 TO 10

Glen Ella Springs is a lovely country inn in the North Georgia mountains, as well as one of Georgia's best restaurants. Owners Barrie and Bobby Aycock shared this never-fail recipe.

Beef Tenderloin

1 (3- to 4-pound) beef tenderloin, trimmed
2 tablespoons salt
1 tablespoon pepper
2 teaspoons celery salt
2 teaspoons onion salt
2/3 cup steak sauce
1/4 cup Worcestershire sauce
Juice of 2 lemons
1/4 cup paprika

Horseradish Sauce

1/4 cup (1/2 stick) butter
2 teaspoons flour
1/4 teaspoon salt
1/4 teaspoon pepper
2/3 cup whipping cream
2 tablespoons horseradish
1 teaspoon Dijon mustard

To prepare the beef, wash the beef and pat dry. Rub the salt, pepper, celery salt and onion salt into the surface of the beef in the order listed. Mix the steak sauce, Worcestershire sauce and lemon juice in a bowl. Rub the sauce into the beef, coating completely. Reserve any remaining sauce. Place the beef in a shallow roasting pan and coat with the paprika. Marinate, covered, in the refrigerator for 8 to 10 hours. Spoon the reserved sauce and any juices in the bottom of the roasting pan over the beef. Roast at 550 degrees for 10 minutes. Reduce the oven temperature to 450 degrees and roast for 8 minutes per pound for medium or until the desired degree of doneness is reached. Remove the beef from the oven and let stand for 10 minutes before carving.

To prepare the sauce, melt the butter in a saucepan over medium heat. Whisk in the flour, salt and pepper. Cook for 1 minute, whisking constantly. Whisk in the cream. Cook for 1 minute or until thick and bubbly, whisking constantly. Stir in the horseradish and Dijon mustard. Serve the sauce with the beef tenderloin.

Pot Roast New Orleans

SERVES 10

1 tablespoon salt
1/2 teaspoon pepper
1/2 teaspoon ground cloves
1/2 teaspoon allspice
1 (4-pound) beef pot roast
1 large onion, chopped
1 garlic clove, finely chopped
1/4 cup vegetable oil
2 tablespoons lemon juice
1 tablespoon white vinegar
3 tablespoons all-purpose flour
1/4 cup vegetable oil
2 (14-ounce) cans whole tomatoes
1 1/2 cups water
2 beef bouillon cubes, crushed
2 or 3 bay leaves
2 onions, sliced
4 carrots, peeled and cut into quarters
4 potatoes, peeled and cut into quarters

Combine the salt, pepper, cloves and allspice in a bowl and mix well. Rub the spice mixture into the surface of the beef, coating evenly. Place the beef in a shallow baking dish. Combine 1 chopped onion, the garlic, 1/4 cup oil, the lemon juice and vinegar in a bowl and mix well. Pour over the beef, turning to coat. Marinate, covered, in the refrigerator for 5 hours, turning occasionally. Remove the beef from the marinade, reserving the marinade. Sprinkle the beef with the flour. Brown in 1/4 cup oil in a large heavy saucepan. Add the reserved marinade, tomatoes, water, bouillon cubes and bay leaves. Simmer, covered, for 2 1/2 hours. Add 2 sliced onions, the carrots and potatoes. Simmer for 45 minutes or until the vegetables are tender. Remove the beef and vegetables to a serving platter. Make gravy if desired by thickening the pan juices with flour.

Very Special Brisket

SERVES ABOUT 20

The history of the Crommelin family of Wetumpka goes back to the early settlement of the area. John G. Crommelin of Harrogate Springs had five sons graduate from the Naval Academy. Pilots Charles and Richard died in World War II. Vice Admiral Henry served on destroyers; Aviator John retired as Rear Admiral; Captain Quentin served as commander at sea. The USS Crommelin *was named in honor of the brothers.*

1/2 teaspoon salt
1/4 teaspoon garlic salt
1 (8- to 10-pound) beef brisket
1/4 cup Worcestershire sauce
1/4 cup soy sauce
1 tablespoon chopped onion
1 teaspoon liquid smoke
1 teaspoon hot red pepper sauce
1/2 teaspoon sugar

Rub the salt and garlic salt into the surface of the beef. Place in a shallow baking dish lined with a double layer of aluminum foil large enough to wrap the beef. Combine the Worcestershire sauce, soy sauce, onion, liquid smoke, hot sauce and sugar. Pour over the beef. Wrap the beef in the aluminum foil, securing the seam and ends well. Marinate in the refrigerator for 24 hours. Bake, wrapped in the foil, at 250 degrees for 10 hours.

Bessie Brand's Camp Stew

MAKES 8 TO 10 GALLONS

If you're going to go to all this trouble, you might as well make a lot. Camp Stew is a highly prized Christmas present in our part of the world. Camp Stew is essentially the same as Brunswick Stew—the name depends on where you live.

20 pounds pork
10 to 20 pounds chicken or turkey
5 to 10 pounds beef
Salt to taste
15 pounds potatoes, coarsely chopped
10 pounds onions, coarsely chopped
1 gallon whole kernel or cream-style corn
1 gallon tomatoes, coarsely chopped
1 gallon ketchup
1 large bottle of Worcestershire sauce, or to taste
Hot red pepper sauce to taste
Minced garlic to taste
Pepper to taste
1/2 cup apple cider vinegar or lemon juice, or to taste
Sugar to taste (optional)

Cook the pork, chicken and beef in boiling salted water to cover in separate large stockpots until the beef is tender and the pork and chicken are cooked through. Drain the meat, reserving the stock in each stockpot. Let the meats and chicken stand until cool enough to handle. Skim any fat from the pork and beef stocks. Remove and discard the bones and fat from the chicken. Chop and shred all of the beef, pork and chicken. Add the potatoes and onions to the beef stock and cook until tender; do not overcook. Add the pork, chicken and beef. Stir in the corn, tomatoes, ketchup, Worcestershire sauce, hot sauce and garlic. Season with salt and pepper. Stir in the pork and chicken stocks. Bring to a gentle simmer and simmer for 3 to 4 hours, stirring frequently. Be careful not to burn. Add the vinegar and sugar in the last 30 minutes of cooking. (**NOTE:** *Other meats or poultry may be substituted and other vegetables such as lima beans and celery may be added. You may use ground beef for the 5 to 10 pounds beef, if desired.)*

Beef Stew

SERVES 6

6 tablespoons shortening, or 3 tablespoons olive oil
3 pounds beef chuck, beef round or beef rump, cut into 1½-inch cubes
2 onions, coarsely chopped
4 cups water
1 cup red wine
2 beef bouillon cubes
2 tablespoons finely chopped parsley
1 garlic clove, finely chopped
1 bay leaf
1½ tablespoons salt
¼ teaspoon pepper
⅛ teaspoon dried thyme
6 potatoes, peeled and cut into halves
6 carrots, peeled and cut into halves
10 white pearl onions
3 ribs celery, cut into 3-inch pieces (optional)
2 green bell peppers, coarsely chopped
4 tomatoes, cut into quarters, or 1 (28-ounce) can tomatoes, cut into quarters
8 ounces mushrooms, sliced (optional)
¼ cup all-purpose flour (optional)
¼ cup water (optional)

Melt the shortening in a stockpot or large heavy saucepan. Add the beef and cook until brown on all sides. Remove the beef, reserving the pan drippings in the pot. Add 2 chopped onions to the pot and sauté until tender. Return the beef to the pot and stir in 4 cups water, the wine, bouillon cubes, parsley, garlic, bay leaf, salt, pepper and thyme. Simmer, covered, for 1 hour and 30 minutes. Add the potatoes, carrots, 10 pearl onions and the celery and cook for 40 minutes. Add the bell peppers, tomatoes, and mushrooms and cook for 20 minutes or until the beef and vegetables are tender.

To prepare a thicker stew, combine the flour and ¼ cup water in a bowl and mix until smooth. Stir quickly into the stew and cook until thickened and bubbly, stirring constantly.

Hot Texas Chili

SERVES 10

2 pounds ground beef
2 pounds chopped beef roast
2 large onions, chopped
2 garlic cloves, chopped
1 jalapeño chile, partially seeded and chopped
4 cups vegetable juice cocktail
1 (28-ounce) can whole tomatoes, coarsely chopped
1 (15-ounce) can tomato sauce
1 (4-ounce) can chopped green chiles
1 (15-ounce) can chili beans, red kidney beans or pinto beans
3 to 5 tablespoons chili powder
1 tablespoon cumin
1 tablespoon celery salt
1 tablespoon pepper

Brown the beef in a stockpot or large heavy saucepan; drain. Add the onions, garlic and jalapeño chile and sauté until the onions are translucent. Stir in the vegetable juice cocktail, undrained tomatoes, tomato sauce, green chiles, beans, chili powder, cumin, celery salt and pepper. Bring to a simmer and simmer for 1 to 2 hours, stirring occasionally.

Old World Lasagna

SERVES 8

1/2 cup finely chopped onion
1 garlic clove, finely chopped
2 tablespoons finely chopped parsley
2 tablespoons olive oil
1 pound ground chuck
8 ounces hot bulk pork sausage
35 ounces canned Italian tomatoes
2 (6-ounce) cans tomato paste
1 tablespoon sugar
1 tablespoon salt
2 teaspoons dried oregano
1 teaspoon dried basil
1/4 teaspoon pepper
3 quarts water
1 tablespoon salt
1 tablespoon vegetable oil
8 ounces lasagna noodles
16 ounces ricotta cheese
1 egg
16 ounces mozzarella cheese, shredded
3 ounces Parmesan cheese, grated

Sauté the onion, garlic and parsley in the olive oil in a large saucepan until the onion is tender. Add the beef and sausage and cook until brown and crumbly, stirring constantly; drain. Stir in the tomatoes, tomato paste, sugar, 1 tablespoon salt, the oregano, basil and pepper. Bring to a boil and reduce the heat to a simmer. Simmer, covered, for 1 to 2 hours, stirring occasionally.

Combine the water, 1 tablespoon salt and the vegetable oil in a large saucepan and bring to boil. Add the noodles two or three at a time. Boil the noodles for 15 minutes or until cooked through. Drain and rinse the noodles under hot water. Combine the ricotta cheese and egg in a small bowl and mix well. Layer the sauce, noodles, ricotta mixture, mozzarella cheese and Parmesan cheese one-third at a time in a greased 9×13-inch baking dish beginning with the sauce. Bake at 350 for 45 to 60 minutes or until bubbly. Let stand for 10 to 15 minutes before serving.

Egyptian Moussaka

SERVES 6

1 1/2 pounds eggplant, peeled and cut into 1/4- to 1/2-inch slices
Salt to taste
All-purpose flour
2 eggs, lightly beaten
1/4 cup vegetable oil
Seasoned bread crumbs
1 pound lean ground beef
2 onions, chopped
1 teaspoon salt
1 teaspoon dried parsley
1 teaspoon cumin
1/2 teaspoon paprika
1/4 teaspoon pepper
1 (6-ounce) can tomato paste
1/2 cup water
1 bay leaf
1/2 cup plain yogurt
2 eggs
2 tablespoons grated Parmesan cheese
1 tablespoon all-purpose flour

Sprinkle the eggplant with salt to taste and let sweat in a colander for 1 hour. Dredge the eggplant in flour, shaking off any excess. Dip in the eggs, coating completely. Fry in batches in the hot oil in a large heavy skillet until golden brown. Drain on paper towels. Dredge in bread crumbs, coating completely. Arrange on a baking sheet and bake at 350 degrees for 20 minutes. Combine the beef, onions, 1 teaspoon salt, the parsley, cumin, paprika and pepper in a large deep skillet and cook until the beef is brown and onions are translucent, stirring occasionally. Stir in the tomato paste, water and bay leaf. Simmer for 10 minutes, stirring occasionally. Discard the bay leaf. Combine the yogurt, eggs, cheese and 1 tablespoon flour in a bowl and mix well. Layer the eggplant and sauce one-third at a time in a 2-quart baking dish. Spread the yogurt mixture on top. Bake at 350 degrees for 30 minutes or until the top is brown.

People have passed through Wetumpka on the De Soto Trail, the Bartram Trail, the annual Wagon Train Ride to the rodeo at the Coliseum in Montgomery, Alabama, the Alabama Antiques Trail along Highway 14, and now the Hank Williams Trail. Some of Ol' Hank's most memorable music was composed at Kowliga on Lake Martin in northwestern Elmore County.

Coca-Cola Ham

SERVES 12

Small handful whole cloves
1 (5- to 8-pound) ham
1 (12-ounce) can Coca-Cola

Press the cloves into the ham. Place the ham skin side up in a deep baking pan or roasting pan. Cook at 350 degrees for 1 hour. Pour half the Coca-Cola over the ham and bake for 30 minutes, basting occasionally. Pour the remaining Coca-Cola over the ham and cook for 30 to 45 minutes or until cooked through, basting occasionally. Serve hot or cold.

Wine-Basted Pork Loin

SERVES 12

3 tablespoons vegetable oil
1 teaspoon dry mustard
1 teaspoon dried whole thyme
1 teaspoon dried marjoram
1 garlic clove, crushed
1 (4- to 5-pound) pork loin
3/4 cup dry white wine

Combine the oil, dry mustard, thyme, marjoram and garlic in a bowl and mix well. Score the pork and rub the marinade over the surface. Wrap the pork in aluminum foil, sealing the seam and ends well. Marinate, in the refrigerator, for 8 hours. Remove from the aluminum foil and place fat side up on a roasting rack in a shallow roasting pan. Bake at 325 degrees for 30 to 35 minutes per pound or until the internal temperature reaches 160 degrees on a meat thermometer, basting frequently with the wine. Let stand for 10 to 15 minutes before carving.

Spanish explorer Hernando DeSoto, probably the first European in Alabama, spent five days in Elmore County in 1540. He is known to have passed through Coosada and to have spent a night near Eclectic. It was DeSoto who introduced hogs to Alabama, for which we are eternally grateful.

Smokin' Grilled Pork Chops

SERVES 6 TO 8

1 cup mayonnaise
2 garlic cloves, finely chopped
2 tablespoons lime juice
2 tablespoons chopped fresh cilantro
1 teaspoon chipotle chili powder
6 to 8 pork chops

Combine the mayonnaise, garlic, lime juice, cilantro and chili powder in a bowl and mix well. Reserve half the sauce. Place the pork chops on a grill rack and grill until cooked through, basting frequently with the remaining sauce. Serve with the reserved sauce. (**NOTE:** *You may also place the pork on a roasting rack in a shallow roasting pan and broil until cooked through, basting frequently with the sauce.)*

Western-Style Pork Chops

SERVES 6

2 tablespoons chili sauce
2 teaspoons Worcestershire sauce
1/2 teaspoon lemon juice
1/2 teaspoon salt
1/4 teaspoon dry mustard
1/4 teaspoon paprika
1/8 teaspoon curry powder
6 (1-inch-thick) pork chops
1/2 cup water

Combine the chili sauce, Worcestershire sauce, lemon juice, salt, dry mustard, paprika and curry powder in a bowl and mix well. Pour the marinade mixture over the pork. Marinate the pork in the refrigerator for 1 hour. Drain the pork, reserving the marinade. Pat the pork dry and brown in a hot greased skillet. Add the water to the marinade and heat in a saucepan, stirring occasionally. Pour over the pork chops. Cook, covered, over medium heat until cooked through or bake at 350 degrees for 1 hour.

Kickin' Boston Butt Roast with Jalapeño Coleslaw

SERVES 10 TO 12

Boston Butt Roast

1 smoked Boston butt roast
1 envelope taco seasoning
1 (14-ounce) can tomatoes
1 (10-ounce) can diced tomatoes with green chiles
1 cup red wine
1 chipotle chile in adobo sauce, seeded
1 teaspoon adobo sauce

Jalapeño Coleslaw

1 package angel hair or finely shredded coleslaw mix
1 jalapeño chile, seeded and cut into quarters
3 green onions
2 tablespoons cider vinegar
1/4 cup mayonnaise, or to taste
Salt and pepper to taste

To prepare the Boston butt roast, place the roast, taco seasoning, tomatoes, tomatoes with green chiles, red wine, chipotle chile and adobo sauce in a slow cooker. Cook a frozen roast on Low for 8 to 10 hours or until the meat falls apart. Cook a thawed roast for 3 to 4 hours or until the meat falls apart, starting on High and reducing the temperature to Low. If the meat doesn't fall apart, shred the meat with a fork. Serve over corn bread or jalapeño coleslaw. (**NOTE:** *Add additional red wine or canned tomatoes if more liquid is needed as the roast cooks.)*

To prepare the coleslaw, pulse the coleslaw mix, jalapeño chile and green onions in food processor until finely chopped. Spoon into a bowl and stir in the vinegar and enough mayonnaise to bind the coleslaw. Season with salt and pepper. Serve with the roast.

Smoked Boston butt roasts are often sold as fund-raisers in our area, especially at our church. This recipe is a great way to feed a crowd if you have a smoked Boston butt roast in the freezer.

It is a great alternative for people who don't like sweet barbecue sauce.

If it ain't pig, it ain't barbecue. We marvel when people call grilling hamburgers "barbecue." Lots of things are good when cooked on the grill, but barbecue translates strictly to pork. The men of Trinity, aka the Butt Brothers, gather monthly to smoke the meat and chew the fat.

Traditional Pork Barbecue

SERVES 8 TO 10

1 (6- to 8-pound) pork shoulder or Boston butt roast
Salt and pepper to taste
1/4 cup (1/2 stick) butter
2 cups apple cider vinegar
2 cups water
3/4 cup Worcestershire sauce
1/2 cup steak sauce
1/4 cup hot red pepper sauce

Prepare and light a charcoal fire in the extreme hot end of a grill that has a hot and a cold end. (The cold end is the one with a vent for smoke to escape.) Burn the charcoal until the coals turn white and grey with no trace of black. Rub the pork liberally with salt and pepper. Place the pork fat side up on a grill rack over indirect heat on the cold side of the grill. Place split pieces of wood or wood chips directly on top of the burning coals. Close the lid of the grill and cook for 2 hours; do not lift the lid. Melt the butter in a saucepan and stir in the vinegar, water, Worcestershire sauce, steak sauce and hot sauce. Open the lid and baste the pork with the sauce. Turn the pork over and baste the top. Close the lid and cook for 2 hours; do not lift the lid. Repeat the basting process. Close the lid and cook for an additional 4 to 6 hours or until the pork is done, basting and turning the pork every hour. (The pork is done when it feels as if it is going to tear in half when twisted from both ends.) Remove the pork from the grill and immediately wrap in aluminum foil. Let stand for 1 hour or longer. Slice or pull the meat apart to serve. (**NOTE:** *The ideal cooking temperature for the grill is around 275 degrees. Cooking more than one pork shoulder will increase the cooking time.)*

Barbecue Pork Ribs

SERVES 4 TO 6

2 cups orange juice or grapefruit juice
1 cup white vinegar
1 tablespoon Worcestershire sauce
1 tablespoon Cajun seasoning
1 tablespoon favorite spice (such as cumin, garlic powder or red pepper flakes)
1 large slab pork ribs
Barbecue sauce (optional)

Combine the orange juice, vinegar, Worcestershire sauce, Cajun seasoning and spice in a bowl and mix well. Cut the membrane from the pork and arrange the ribs in a shallow baking dish. Pour the orange juice mixture over the pork, turning to coat completely. Marinate, covered, in the refrigerator for 8 to 10 hours, turning occasionally. Light one side of a grill and heat to 250 degrees. Place the ribs on a grill rack on the opposite side of the grill. Cook, with the grill lid down, for 1 hour, turning every 15 minutes. Remove the pork from the grill and wrap in aluminum foil. Return to the grill. Cook for 4 to 5 hours, rotating every hour. Rub the pork with barbecue sauce and rewrap in the aluminum foil if desired during the last hour of cooking.

Rib Rub

MAKES ENOUGH FOR 2 SLABS OF RIBS

1/2 cup packed brown sugar
1/4 cup paprika
1 tablespoon black pepper
1 tablespoon salt
1 tablespoon chili powder
3/4 tablespoon onion powder
3/4 tablespoon garlic powder
1 teaspoon cayenne pepper

Combine the brown sugar, paprika, black pepper, salt, chili powder, onion powder, garlic powder and cayenne pepper in a bowl and mix well. Rub into pork ribs before grilling.

Red Beans and Rice

SERVES 8

Louis Armstrong loved this dish so much he signed his correspondence "Red beans and ricely yours."

11 1/2 cups water
1 pound dried red beans, rinsed and sorted
1 ham bone
2 teaspoons garlic salt
1 teaspoon Worcestershire sauce
1/4 teaspoon Tabasco sauce
1 cup chopped celery
1 cup chopped onion
1 1/2 garlic cloves, minced
3 tablespoons vegetable oil
8 ounces ham, cut into cubes
8 ounces smoked sausage, sliced
4 ounces hot sausage, sliced
2 bay leaves
Salt and coarsely ground pepper to taste
1/4 cup chopped parsley
2 cups hot cooked rice

Combine the water, beans, ham bone, garlic salt, Worcestershire sauce and Tabasco sauce in a large heavy saucepan or stockpot. Cook, uncovered, over low heat. Sauté the celery, onion and garlic in the hot oil in a skillet until transparent; set aside. Sauté the ham, smoked sausage and hot sausage in a skillet until brown; drain. Stir the ham, sausage, bay leaves, salt and pepper into the beans. Cook for 2 1/2 hours or until the beans are tender and the desired consistency is reached. Discard the bay leaves. Stir in the parsley and adjust seasonings if needed. Serve over the rice and top with the onion mixture if desired. (**NOTE:** *This recipe can be tripled, using 3 pounds dried red kidney beans and adding a variety of meat, including pan sausage and kielbasa. You may add bell peppers to the onion mixture before sautéing. You may use barley instead of the rice. This dish freezes well.)*

First-Place Barbecue Sauce

MAKES 2 1/2 TO 3 QUARTS

4 cups apple cider vinegar
2 cups (4 sticks) butter
3 cups ketchup
1 (10-ounce) bottle Worcestershire sauce
1 1/2 cups mustard
1 tablespoon salt
1 tablespoon pepper
Dash of Tabasco sauce

Combine the vinegar, butter, ketchup, Worcestershire sauce, mustard, salt, pepper and Tabasco sauce in a saucepan and bring to a boil, stirring occasionally. Let stand until completely cool. Pour into bottles and seal with lids. Refrigerate until ready to use. (**NOTE:** *Whiskey bottles are recommended for storing this sauce. Do not wash out the bottles; a few drops of whisky should remain in the bottles when filled with the sauce. This sauce keeps for up to 6 months in the refrigerator.)*

Tangy Barbecue Sauce

SERVES 1 QUART

3 cups ketchup
1 cup dill pickle juice
1 to 3 tablespoons brown sugar
3 garlic cloves, crushed, or 1 tablespoon garlic powder
1 tablespoon yellow mustard
1 tablespoon hot red pepper sauce, or to taste
1 teaspoon Worcestershire sauce
1/2 teaspoon pepper

Combine the ketchup, pickle juice, brown sugar, garlic, mustard, hot sauce, Worcestershire sauce and pepper in a saucepan and bring to a simmer. Simmer for 12 to 15 minutes, stirring occasionally. Let stand until completely cool. Store in bottles in the refrigerator.

ALABAMA NATIVES, ALABAMA NEIGHBORS

The Creek Indians of Alabama probably descended from the Mississippian culture that existed in Alabama almost 1,000 years ago. The Mississippians built massive earthen mounds including those where the Coosa and Tallapoosa join to form the Alabama River just south of Wetumpka.

The Creek Confederacy consisted of much of what is now west Georgia and east Alabama. They lived along the rivers from Wetumpka to Tensaw with a major center of activity at the Coosa-Tallapoosa juncture, near Fort Toulouse.

In 1790, the Creeks gave the U.S. government permission to use and improve the Indian trail through Alabama. The trail became the Federal Road, giving settlers access to the newly purchased Louisiana Territory. Creeks built businesses along the route and served as guides and interpreters to settlers passing through.

As settlers encroached on Indian lands, tensions grew and eventually culminated in the Creek Indian War. When the Creeks were defeated in 1814 at Horseshoe Bend, Andrew Jackson built Fort Jackson on the site of old Fort Toulouse.

In 1984, the Poarch Creeks gained official tribal recognition from the U.S. Bureau of Indian Affairs, making the Tribe a sovereign nation. Today they own three gaming facilities in Alabama, including the Riverside Entertainment Center in Wetumpka.

This section was generously sponsored by

ALABAMA POULTRY AND EGG ASSOCIATION

Poultry Main Dishes

WHEN FRIENDS

GATHER 'ROUND FROM

AFAR DO WE NOT

REJOICE?

EASTERN PROVERB

Ruth Stovall's Chicken Artichoke Casserole

SERVES 8 TO 10

On the first Saturday of every month, except January and February, the open-air flea market in Santuck is a famous gathering place. From predawn to mid-afternoon, venders sell food, antiques, incredible plants, crafts, junk, socks, and assorted other stuff. Some plan their lives around being there early, and everybody needs to experience it at least once.

2 (10-ounce) cans cream of chicken soup
1 cup mayonnaise
1/3 cup white wine
1 teaspoon lemon juice
1/4 teaspoon curry powder
1 (14-ounce) can artichoke hearts, drained
3 to 4 cups chopped cooked chicken
1 1/2 cups (6 ounces) shredded Cheddar cheese
1 1/4 cups buttered bread crumbs
2 tablespoons butter, melted

Combine the soup, mayonnaise, wine, lemon juice and curry powder in a bowl and blend until smooth. Arrange the artichokes in a 9×12-inch baking dish. Layer the chicken over the artichokes. Pour the soup mixture evenly over the top and sprinkle with the cheese. Top with the bread crumbs and drizzle with the butter. Bake at 350 degrees for 25 minutes. (**NOTE:** *This casserole may be stored, covered, in the refrigerator or freezer before adding the bread crumbs. If frozen, thaw and let stand to reach room temperature before proceeding as directed above.)*

No-Pasta Chicken Casserole

SERVES 6

8 ounces mushrooms, sliced
1/2 cup chopped onion
1 teaspoon crushed garlic
2 tablespoons butter, melted
3 cups chopped cooked chicken
1 (12-ounce) can artichoke hearts, drained and sliced
1 (5-ounce) can sliced water chestnuts, drained
1 (4-ounce) jar sliced pimentos, drained
3/4 cup mayonnaise
1/2 cup sour cream
1/2 cup chicken broth
1 cup plus 2 to 3 tablespoons grated Parmesan cheese

Sauté the mushrooms, onion and garlic in the butter in a skillet until tender. Remove from the heat. Add the chicken, artichokes, water chestnuts and pimentos and mix well. Combine the mayonnaise, sour cream and broth and blend until smooth. Stir in 1 cup of the cheese. Add the chicken mixture and stir until well combined. Spoon into a greased 8×12-inch baking dish. Sprinkle the remaining 2 to 3 tablespoons cheese on top. Bake at 350 degrees for 20 minutes. (**NOTE:** *This casserole may be made ahead. Chill, covered, in the refrigerator until ready to bake. Increase the baking time to 1 hour.)*

Chicken in Basil Sauce

SERVES 4

If you are frying or sautéing meat or poultry, always pat the surface dry with paper towels. If you don't, the water will boil and the meat or poultry will not brown well.

2 tablespoons butter
1/4 teaspoon salt
1/4 teaspoon coarse ground pepper
4 (6-ounce) boneless skinless chicken breasts, left whole or cut into bite-size pieces
1 tablespoon all-purpose flour
1 cup regular or fat-free half-and-half
2 teaspoons finely chopped garlic
1 large tomato, coarsely chopped, or 1 small yellow tomato and 1 small red tomato, coarsely chopped
1/4 cup fresh basil leaves, chopped, or 2 tablespoons dried basil
Hot cooked pasta
Fresh basil leaves
Tomato slices

Melt the butter in a 10-inch skillet until sizzling. Stir in the salt and pepper. Add the chicken and cook over medium-high heat for 8 to 10 minutes or until golden brown, turning once. Remove the chicken and set aside. Stir the flour into the pan drippings until combined. Add the half-and-half and garlic and cook for 1 minute or until slightly thickened, stirring constantly. Stir in the tomato and basil. Return the chicken to the skillet and cook for 4 to 5 minutes until the chicken is cooked through. Serve over pasta. Garnish with basil and tomato slices.

Chilled Chicken Elise

SERVES 3 TO 6

Chicken

3/4 cup white wine
6 tablespoons chopped fresh parsley
3 tablespoons butter
6 peppercorns
1 bay leaf
6 boneless skinless chicken breasts

Green Peppercorn Sauce

2 egg yolks
2 tablespoons Dijon mustard
2 tablespoons white wine
2 teaspoons sugar
1/2 teaspoon salt
1/4 teaspoon white pepper
2 tablespoons green peppercorns in brine, drained and rinsed
1 tablespoon butter
1/2 cup heavy whipping cream

To prepare the chicken, combine the wine, parsley, butter, peppercorns and bay leaf in a deep skillet. Bring to a simmer. Add the chicken and enough water to barely cover. Return to a gentle simmer and simmer for 7 to 10 minutes or until the chicken is just cooked through; do not overcook. Remove the chicken from the poaching liquid to a platter. Chill, covered, in the refrigerator.

To prepare the sauce, combine the egg yolks, Dijon mustard, wine, sugar, salt and white pepper in a double boiler. Cook over hot (not boiling) water for 5 minutes or until thickened, stirring constantly. Remove from the heat and stir in the green peppercorns and butter. Whip the cream until stiff peaks form and fold into the sauce. Chill, covered, in the refrigerator for 8 hours or until ready to serve.

To serve, place the chilled chicken on a serving platter or individual plates and spoon the green peppercorn sauce on top. (**NOTE:** *The sauce will keep for one week in the refrigerator.)*

William Bartram, renowned artist, naturalist, and botanist for King George of England, traveled through Elmore County during the Revolutionary War. He described Fort Toulouse as "one of the most eligible situations for a city in the world." You can walk along the Bartram Trail in Fort Toulouse-Jackson Park.

Baked Chicken

SERVES 2 TO 4

2 to 4 boneless skinless chicken breasts
1/4 cup mayonnaise
Cracker crumbs or seasoned bread crumbs
2 to 4 tablespoons butter, melted

Coat the chicken in the mayonnaise. Marinate, covered, in the refrigerator for 30 minutes. Press into cracker crumbs, coating completely. Place on a greased baking sheet and drizzle with the butter. Bake at 350 degrees for 30 minutes or until the chicken is cooked through. (**NOTE:** *You may substitute 1/2 to 1 cup sour cream mixed with 1/4 cup lemon juice for the mayonnaise.)*

Easy Chicken Pie

SERVES 6

1 whole chicken, or 4 chicken breasts
1 (10-ounce) can cream of chicken soup
1 cup buttermilk
1 cup self-rising flour
1/2 cup (1 stick) butter or margarine, melted
1 1/2 cups green peas
1 1/2 cups cooked carrots
1 (7-ounce) can corn niblets (optional)
Salt and pepper to taste

Boil the chicken in water to cover in a large saucepan or stockpot until cooked through. Drain, reserving 3/4 cup of the cooking liquid. Remove and discard the skin and bones. Chop the chicken. Combine the reserved cooking liquid, soup, buttermilk, flour and butter in a bowl and whisk until smooth. Layer the chicken, peas, carrots and corn in a 9×13-inch baking dish sprayed with nonstick cooking spray. Sprinkle with salt and pepper. Pour the soup mixture over the top. Bake at 400 degrees for 30 to 40 minutes or until light brown and bubbly.

Fiesta Chicken Salad

Makes 24 cups

3 pounds boneless skinless chicken breasts
6 tomatoes, chopped
3 avocados, chopped
2 zucchini, cut lengthwise into halves and sliced
2 cups frozen corn, thawed
1 1/2 cups picante sauce
1/4 cup chopped cilantro
3 tablespoons lemon juice
1 tablespoon vegetable oil
1 1/2 teaspoons garlic powder
1 1/2 teaspoons cumin
Salt and pepper to taste
Lettuce leaves
Lemon slices, radish roses and green onions

Grill the chicken on a grill rack until cooked through. Let stand until cool and then chop. Combine the chicken, tomatoes, avocados, zucchini and corn in a large bowl and mix well. Mix the picante sauce, cilantro, lemon juice, oil, garlic powder, cumin, salt and pepper in a bowl. Pour over the chicken mixture and toss until completely coated. Chill, covered, until ready to serve. Serve in large bowls lined with lettuce leaves. Garnish with lemon slices, radish roses and green onions.

Old-Fashioned Chicken Salad

Makes 8 cups

1 whole chicken
1 rib celery
1/2 onion
8 hard-cooked eggs
Salt and pepper to taste
1 (4-ounce) jar sweet pickle relish
Mayonnaise to taste

Boil the chicken in water to cover in a large saucepan or stockpot until cooked through; drain. Let stand until completely cool. Remove and discard the bones and skin. Chop the celery in a food processor. Drain the liquid. Add the onion and process until chopped. Add the chicken and eggs and process until combined. Season with salt and pepper. Add the undrained pickle relish and mayonnaise and process until combined. Spoon the mixture into a bowl. Chill, covered, in the refrigerator for 1 hour.

Maple Chicken Salad

SERVES 10

2 cups chopped cooked chicken
2 tablespoons maple syrup
1 cup mayonnaise
1 garlic clove, minced
1/2 teaspoon dry mustard
1/2 teaspoon Worcestershire sauce
1/4 teaspoon pepper
3 cups loosely packed shredded lettuce
2 cups loosely packed shredded spinach
1 cup frozen English peas, thawed
1 red bell pepper, chopped
2 green onions, chopped
1 cup (4 ounces) shredded Cheddar cheese
1/2 cup dry-roasted peanuts

Toss the chicken with the maple syrup in a bowl until coated. Combine the mayonnaise, garlic, dry mustard, Worcestershire sauce and pepper in a bowl and mix well. Layer half the lettuce and half the spinach in a 4 1/2-quart salad bowl. Layer with the peas, bell pepper, chicken mixture and green onions. Top with the remaining lettuce and spinach. Sprinkle with the cheese. Spread the mayonnaise mixture over the top, sealing to the edge. Chill, covered, for 8 hours. Toss just before serving. Sprinkle with the peanuts.

Grilled Chicken and Peach Salad

SERVES 4

Peach Salad Dressing

1 peach, peeled and chopped
1 cup white wine vinegar
2 tablespoons sugar
1 tablespoon Dijon mustard
1 teaspoon salt
1 cup olive oil

Salad

4 boneless skinless chicken breasts
4 peaches, peeled and cut into halves
2 tablespoons olive oil
1 teaspoon salt
1/2 teaspoon pepper
2 cups mixed salad greens
1/2 cup chopped celery
1/2 cup chopped pecans or slivered almonds, toasted
1/4 cup sliced green onions

To prepare the dressing, process the peach, vinegar, sugar, Dijon mustard and salt in a blender. Add the olive oil gradually, processing constantly at low speed until incorporated.

To prepare the salad, brush the chicken and peaches with the olive oil. Season the chicken with the salt and pepper. Place the chicken on a grill rack and grill until cooked through. Place the peaches cut side down on a grill rack and grill for 3 minutes or until lightly charred. Let the chicken and peaches stand until cool. Slice one peach and set aside. Chop the chicken and remaining three peaches and place in a large salad bowl. Add the salad greens, celery, pecans and green onions. Add the dressing and toss until well coated. Divide among four salad plates. Garnish with reserved peach slices. (**NOTE:** *This salad dressing is great on any fruit salad.)*

Jamaican Chicken Stew

SERVES 4 TO 6

1 cup long grain rice
1 pound boneless skinless chicken breasts, cut into bite-size pieces
1 teaspoon curry powder
1 teaspoon dried thyme
1/2 teaspoon ground allspice
1/2 teaspoon cracked black pepper
1/4 to 1/2 teaspoon crushed red pepper
1 cup chopped onion
1 1/2 teaspoons jarred minced garlic
2 teaspoons olive oil
1 (15-ounce) can black beans, drained and rinsed
1 (14-ounce) can diced tomatoes
1/4 cup dry red wine
2 tablespoons capers, drained
1 or 2 sweet potatoes, baked and cut into bite-size pieces

Prepare the rice according to the package directions, omitting the salt and grease. Combine the chicken, curry powder, thyme, allspice, black pepper and red pepper in a bowl and mix well. Sauté the onion and garlic in the hot olive oil in a large deep skillet over medium-high heat for 3 minutes or until tender. Add the chicken mixture and sauté for 4 minutes. Stir in the black beans, tomatoes, wine and capers. Cover and reduce the heat. Simmer for 10 minutes or until the chicken is cooked through. Add the sweet potatoes and simmer until the sweet potatoes are heated through. Serve over the rice. (**NOTE:** *You may substitute pork for the chicken.)*

Mediterranean-Style Chicken

SERVES 8

8 (5-ounce) boneless skinless chicken breasts
1/4 cup all-purpose flour
1/4 cup olive oil
1 red onion, chopped
1/4 cup (1/2 stick) butter
2 garlic cloves, chopped
4 Roma tomatoes, chopped
1 cup green olives, sliced
1/2 cup black olives, sliced
1/4 cup capers, drained
10 fresh basil leaves
1 cup white wine
8 ounces feta cheese, crumbled

Pound the chicken to 1/4-inch thickness. Dredge the chicken in the flour, shaking off any excess. Cook the chicken in the hot olive oil in a deep skillet until cooked through and brown on all sides. Remove the chicken from the pan and arrange in a baking dish. Add the red onion, butter and garlic to the pan drippings in the skillet and sauté until the onions are tender. Add the tomatoes, green olives, black olives, capers and basil and cook until the tomatoes begin to soften. Add the wine and deglaze the pan. Pour over the chicken. Sprinkle with the cheese. Bake at 350 degrees for 30 minutes.

Chicken and Sun-Dried Tomatoes

SERVES 6 TO 8

1 (3-ounce) package sun-dried tomatoes
Boiling water
6 to 8 boneless skinless chicken breasts
2 tablespoons butter, melted
2 large shallots, chopped
6 large mushrooms, sliced
2/3 cup heavy cream
1/4 cup vermouth or dry white wine
2 tablespoons Dijon mustard
2 tablespoons tarragon

Place the sun-dried tomatoes in a heatproof bowl. Add boiling water to cover and let stand for 2 minutes or until the sun-dried tomatoes are soft; drain. Cut the sun-dried tomatoes into strips; set aside. Pound the chicken with a mallet until flat and tender. Brown the chicken in the butter in a skillet. Remove the chicken to a plate. Add the shallots and mushrooms to the pan drippings and sauté until tender. Add the cream, vermouth, Dijon mustard and tarragon and simmer until the sauce thickens, stirring occasionally. Add the chicken and cook until the chicken is cooked through. Serve with pasta or rice. (**NOTE:** *You may substitute veal or shrimp for the chicken.)*

The chicken auction that takes place near Eclectic every Friday night is not limited to chickens. You may also purchase goats, rabbits, and every known variety of fowl at this memorable gathering.

Chicken Supreme

SERVES 6 TO 8

4 boneless skinless chicken breasts
1 (10-ounce) can cream of chicken soup
1 (10-ounce) can cream of mushroom soup
2 cups sour cream
2 (8-ounce) cans water chestnuts
Cracker crumbs

Boil the chicken in water to cover in a large saucepan until cooked through; drain. Let the chicken stand until cool. Chop the chicken and place in a large bowl. Add the chicken soup, mushroom soup, sour cream and water chestnuts and mix well. Press cracker crumbs 1/2 inch thick in a 9×13-inch baking dish. Spoon the chicken mixture over the cracker crumbs and spread evenly to the edges. Top with cracker crumbs measuring 1/2 inch thick. Bake at 350 degrees for 45 minutes or until bubbly.

Chicken and Wild Rice

Serves 20 to 24

1 (32-ounce) package long grain and wild rice garden blend mix (available at restaurant supply stores)
6 cups chopped cooked chicken
4 (16-ounce) cans French-style green beans
4 (10-ounce) cans cream of celery soup
4 cups mayonnaise
2 (8-ounce) cans sliced water chestnuts
2 onions, chopped
Salt and pepper to taste
Paprika
Chopped parsley

Cook the rice according to the package directions. Combine the rice, chicken, green beans, soup, mayonnaise, water chestnuts and onions in a bowl and mix well. Season with salt and pepper. Spoon into a large baking dish. Sprinkle with paprika and parsley. Bake at 350 degrees for 30 minutes or until heated through and bubbly.

I EATS ME SPINACH

You cannot overestimate the importance of the Coosa River in the history of Wetumpka and Elmore County, but few people know that the Coosa can claim one of the world's most famous sailors. In 1913 when the U.S. Corps of Engineers completed a lock and dam on the river to make navigation possible over the Horseleg Shoals, they bought a boat to keep the channel navigable. The Leota *was a beautiful steamboat, but only used for construction and dredging channels. The captain of the* Leota *was a Mr. Sims of Ohatchee, Alabama. His son Tom grew up on the Coosa and loved it.*

Tom was a gifted cartoonist and began drawing the comic strip "Thimble Theater" when creator Elzie Segar died in 1938. The cartoon was about a shipping family by the name of Oyl. Commodore Oyl, the father, has a son named Castor and a daughter named Olive. Popeye was one of the sailors who worked for the shipping company. Tom took this character and spun off the comic strip "Popeye."

Tom Sims said, "Fantastic as Popeye is, the whole story is based on facts. As a boy I was raised on the Coosa River. When I began writing the script for 'Popeye' I put my characters back on the old Leota *I knew as a boy, transformed it into a ship, and made the Coosa River a salty sea."*

This section was generously sponsored by

RIVER BANK AND TRUST

Seafood Main Dishes

I GATHER ROSES

FROM THORNS,

GOLD FROM

THE EARTH,

THE PEARL FROM

THE OYSTER.

JEROME, ROMAN
CHURCH FATHER

Crab au Gratin

SERVES 4 TO 6

Did you know you could make a white sauce in the microwave? Place the butter in a microwave-safe dish. Microwave on High for 30 to 60 seconds or until melted. Whisk in the flour. Microwave on High for 1 minute. Whisk in the liquid gradually. Microwave on High at 1-minute intervals until thickened to the desired consistency, stirring after each interval. The liquid will be determined by the consistency of the sauce that you wish to make: thin, medium, or thick.

5 tablespoons butter
3 tablespoons all-purpose flour
1 cup half-and-half
1 cup chicken broth
1 egg, beaten
1 tablespoon sherry
1 tablespoon Worcestershire sauce
1 teaspoon salt
1 teaspoon white pepper
1/2 teaspoon Old Bay seasoning
Dash of Tabasco sauce
1 pound crab meat, flaked
1 cup (4 ounces) shredded Cheddar cheese

Melt the butter in a saucepan over low heat. Add the flour and cook for 2 minutes, stirring constantly; do not brown. Add the half-and-half gradually, stirring constantly. Cook over low heat until thickened, stirring constantly.

Add the chicken broth and egg to the white sauce and cook for 1 minute, stirring constantly. Remove from the heat and stir in the sherry, Worcestershire sauce, salt, white pepper, Old Bay seasoning and Tabasco sauce. Fold in the crab meat. Spoon into a 1 1/2-quart baking dish or six ramekins. Sprinkle with the cheese. Bake at 350 degrees for 20 minutes.

Rice and Crab Romanoff

SERVES 5

2 cups hot cooked rice
1/2 cup creamed cottage cheese
1 (2-ounce) can sliced mushrooms, drained
2 tablespoons chopped chives
1/4 cup sour cream
1/4 cup mayonnaise
1/2 teaspoon Worcestershire sauce
1/2 teaspoon salt
1/8 teaspoon cayenne pepper
1/8 teaspoon black pepper
2 tablespoons grated Parmesan cheese
1 (7-ounce) can lump crab meat
Paprika

Combine the rice, cottage cheese, mushrooms and chives in a large bowl and mix well. Combine the sour cream, mayonnaise, Worcestershire sauce, salt, cayenne pepper, black pepper and 1 tablespoon of the Parmesan cheese in a bowl and mix well. Fold into the rice mixture. Fold in the crab meat, being careful not to break up the lumps. Spoon into a buttered shallow 1-quart baking dish. Top with the remaining 1 tablespoon Parmesan cheese and sprinkle with paprika. Bake at 350 degrees for 25 minutes or until heated through.

Oysters Rockefeller Casserole

SERVES 10

3 (10-ounce) packages frozen chopped spinach, thawed and drained
1 2/3 cups chopped green onions
1 cup chopped celery
1 large garlic clove, crushed
1 teaspoon thyme
1 1/2 cups (3 sticks) butter, melted
1 1/2 cups bread crumbs
1 tablespoon Worcestershire sauce
1 teaspoon anchovy paste
4 dozen small oysters
1/2 cup oyster liquor
3/4 cup chopped parsley
1/2 cup (2 ounces) grated Parmesan cheese
2 tablespoons Pernod (anise-flavored liqueur)
1/2 teaspoon salt
1/4 teaspoon black pepper
1/4 teaspoon cayenne pepper

Cook the spinach according to the package instructions; drain. Sauté the green onions, celery, garlic and thyme in the butter in a skillet for 5 minutes. Add the bread crumbs, Worcestershire sauce and anchovy paste and cook for 5 minutes or until the bread crumbs are toasted, stirring constantly. Fold in the oysters, oyster liquor, parsley, cheese and liqueur. Cook for 3 minutes or until the edges of the oysters curl. Add the spinach, salt, black pepper and cayenne pepper and stir well. Spoon in a 3-quart casserole. Bake at 375 degrees for 20 to 25 minutes. (**NOTE:** *This dish may be baked in ramekins and served as appetizers.)*

Oysters Saint Louis

SERVES 6 TO 8

1 pound mushrooms, chopped
Melted butter for sautéing
1 bunch green onions, finely chopped
2 cups red wine
1 bay leaf
Salt and pepper to taste
1 (14-ounce) can artichoke,
cut into 1/8-inch pieces
1/2 cup black olives, chopped
3 dozen oysters

Sauté the mushrooms in butter in a skillet until tender. Add the green onions, wine and bay leaf. Season with salt and pepper and reduce by half. Add the artichokes and olives. Arrange the oysters in a baking dish or ramekins and spoon the sauce evenly over the top. Bake at 375 degrees for 15 to 20 minutes or until the oysters reach the desired degree of doneness.

Big Fish, *a Tim Burton movie starring the likes of Jessica Lange, Albert Finney, Danny DeVito, and Ewan McGregor, made a big splash when it was filmed in our town on our bridge and along our river. If you haven't seen it, take a look.*

Barbecue Shrimp

Serves 6 to 8

Fish to taste right, must swim three times—in water, in butter, and in wine.
—Polish Proverb

2 cups (4 sticks) butter
1/2 cup white wine
4 garlic cloves, crushed
2 bay leaves, crumbled
2 tablespoons Worcestershire sauce
Juice of 1 lemon
1 tablespoon dried oregano
1 teaspoon dried rosemary
1 teaspoon barbecue spice or seafood seasoning
Salt and pepper to taste
Tabasco sauce to taste
5 pounds unpeeled (15- to 20-count) shrimp

Combine the butter, wine, garlic, bay leaves, Worcestershire sauce, lemon juice, oregano, rosemary and barbecue spice in a large heavy saucepan. Season with salt, pepper and Tabasco sauce and bring to a simmer. Add the shrimp and mix well. Cover with a lid and simmer for 15 minutes. Uncover and simmer for an additional 15 minutes. Remove from the heat and let stand for 3 to 4 minutes. Spoon the shrimp and sauce into individual serving bowls. Serve with hot crusty bread for dipping.

Black Pepper Shrimp

SERVES 4

2 pounds unpeeled shrimp
1 (1-ounce) container pepper
1 cup (2 sticks) butter or margarine, cut into pieces

Place the shrimp in shallow baking pan. Cover with the black pepper. Dot evenly with the butter. Bake, covered, at 400 degrees until the tops of the shrimp begin to turn pink. Turn the shrimp and cook until pink. Remove the shrimp from the oven and toss in the pan juices. Peel and eat hot. (**NOTE:** *Because the shrimp are cooked in their shells, they get the flavor of the black pepper without the heat.)*

Biloxi Boiled Shrimp

SERVES 8 TO 10

1 or 2 (3-ounce) bags shrimp boil
1 cup rock salt
1 onion
1 lemon, cut into halves
3 garlic cloves
Black pepper to taste
Cayenne pepper to taste
10 pounds shrimp

Combine the shrimp boil, rock salt, onion, lemon, garlic, black pepper, cayenne pepper and enough water to cover the shrimp in a large stockpot and bring to a boil. Add the shrimp and return to a boil. Boil for 3 to 5 minutes or until the shrimp turn pink. Remove the shrimp with a slotted spoon to a colander and toss immediately with ice cubes to stop the cooking process. Discard the contents of the stockpot. Serve with toasted French bread. (**NOTE:** *Add corn on the cob, new potatoes and sliced link sausage for a one-pot feast.)*

Casa Napoli Blackened Shrimp Caesar Salad

SERVES 1

Casa Napoli brought excellent Italian cuisine to an interesting location on the south rim of the Wetumpka Crater.

Salad
3 ounces shrimp, peeled and deveined
3 tablespoons butter, melted
Blackening seasoning to taste
Chopped romaine
Shredded mozzarella cheese
Shredded provolone cheese
Chopped red onion
Chopped Roma tomato
Toasted slivered almonds
Shaved Parmesan cheese

Caesar Dressing
2 pasteurized eggs
4 anchovy fillets, mashed
2 garlic cloves, minced
2 tablespoons lemon juice
1 teaspoon Worcestershire sauce
Salt and pepper to taste
1/3 cup olive oil

To prepare the salad, sauté the shrimp in the butter in a skillet over high heat for 2 minutes or until the shrimp begin to turn pink. Add blackening seasoning and saute for 1 minute or until the shrimp turn completely pink. Remove from the heat. Toss the lettuce with the dressing in a bowl, coating completely. Arrange on a salad plate. Layer with mozzarella cheese, provolone cheese, onion, tomato and the shrimp. Sprinkle with almonds and Parmesan cheese.

To prepare the dressing, cook the eggs in boiling water to cover in a saucepan for 45 seconds. Peel the eggs, discard the whites and place the yolks in a small bowl. Add the anchovies, garlic, lemon juice and Worcestershire sauce and whisk until combined. Season with salt and pepper. Add the olive oil in a fine stream, whisking constantly until incorporated. Use immediately.

Angel Hair Pasta with Shrimp and Goat Cheese

SERVES 4 TO 6

1 cup chopped onion
3/4 cup chopped green bell pepper
3 teaspoons crushed garlic
1 tablespoon olive oil
1 (14-ounce) can diced tomatoes
1 (10-ounce) can diced tomatoes with green chiles
2 teaspoons capers, drained
2 teaspoons dried basil
2 teaspoons dried oregano
1/2 teaspoon chili flakes
4 ounces goat cheese, crumbled
1 pound shrimp, peeled
Hot cooked angel hair pasta

Sauté the onion, bell pepper and garlic in the hot olive oil in a nonstick skillet until tender. Add the tomatoes, tomatoes with green chiles, capers, basil, oregano and chili flakes and simmer for 30 minutes, stirring occasionally. Add the cheese and cook for 1 minute or until melted and well combined, stirring constantly. Add the shrimp and cook until the shrimp turn pink, stirring occasionally. Serve over angel hair pasta in pasta bowls.

Tecumseh, daring chief of the Shawnees, came into this area to urge the Creeks to join an Indian confederacy.

Greek Island Shrimp

SERVES 4 TO 6

1 large green bell pepper, cut into 1/2-inch pieces
8 ounces mushrooms, sliced
1/2 cup minced onion
2 tablespoons olive oil
2 tablespoons butter, melted
1 cup dry white wine
4 tomatoes, peeled and chopped
1 small garlic clove, minced
1 teaspoon oregano
1 teaspoon salt
1/2 teaspoon pepper
8 ounces feta cheese, crumbled
1 pound large shrimp, peeled and deveined
1 cup pitted black olives, sliced
2 tablespoons ouzo
1/2 cup chopped fresh parsley

Sauté the bell pepper, mushrooms and onion in the hot olive oil and butter until the vegetables are tender. Stir in the wine, tomatoes, garlic, oregano, salt and pepper and bring to a boil. Lower the heat to medium and simmer until the sauce is slightly thickened. Stir in the cheese and simmer for 10 to 15 minutes. Add the shrimp and olives. Cook for 5 minutes or until the shrimp turn pink; do not overcook the shrimp. Stir in the ouzo. Spoon into large individual serving bowls. Garnish evenly with the parsley. Serve crusty French bread on the side.

Penne Pasta with Shrimp and Squash

SERVES 6

4 cups thinly sliced yellow squash
3 cups thinly sliced zucchini
2 tablespoons olive oil
1 pound medium shrimp, peeled and deveined
1/4 cup fresh lemon juice
3 garlic cloves, minced
1 teaspoon dried basil
1 teaspoon dried oregano
1/2 teaspoon salt
1/4 teaspoon pepper
4 cups hot cooked penne (about 8 ounces uncooked)
1/2 cup thinly sliced fresh chives or green onions
1/4 cup (1 ounce) freshly grated Parmesan cheese

Sauté the squash and zucchini in the hot olive oil in a skillet over medium-high heat for 10 minutes. Add the shrimp and sauté for 3 minutes. Add the lemon juice, garlic, basil, oregano, salt and pepper and sauté until the shrimp turn pink. Combine the shrimp mixture, pasta, chives and cheese in a large serving bowl and toss gently to combine.

Shrimp and Wild Rice Casserole

SERVES 6 TO 8

If you must wash mushrooms, do so quickly under running water and dry immediately. Mushrooms absorb water. This can be disastrous if you wish to sauté them.

1 1/2 pounds mushrooms, sliced
1 small bell pepper, chopped
1/4 cup chopped onion
1/4 cup (1/2 stick) butter, melted
2 pounds shrimp, peeled and deveined
3 cups cooked wild rice
2 (10-ounce) cans cream of mushroom soup
1/2 cup half-and-half
1 garlic clove, minced
1 tablespoon Worcestershire sauce
1/4 teaspoon thyme
Salt and pepper to taste
1 cup (4 ounces) shredded Monterey Jack cheese

Sauté the mushrooms, bell pepper and onion in the butter in a skillet until the vegetables are tender. Add the shrimp and sauté until the shrimp turn pink. Remove from the heat and stir in the wild rice, soup, half-and-half, garlic, Worcestershire sauce and thyme. Season with salt and pepper. Spoon into a greased baking dish. Sprinkle with the cheese. Bake at 350 degrees for 30 to 45 minutes. (**NOTE:** *You may divide the casserole between two greased baking dishes. Store one, covered, in the freezer for later use.)*

Savory Shrimp and Chicken Casserole

SERVES 8

6 to 8 chicken breasts
1 cup finely chopped onion
1 cup finely chopped celery
2 tablespoons dried parsley, or
1/4 cup chopped fresh parsley
2 tablespoons butter, melted
2 pounds cooked peeled shrimp
2 cups mayonnaise
2 cups shredded pumpernickel bread
1 cup shredded white bread
2 tablespoons mustard
2 tablespoons capers, drained
2 teaspoons Worcestershire sauce
1/2 teaspoon curry powder

Boil the chicken in water to cover in a large saucepan until cooked through. Drain the chicken, reserving 1 cup of the cooking liquid. Let the chicken stand until cool enough to handle. Discard the skin and bones. Chop the chicken into bite-size pieces. Sauté the onion, celery and parsley in the butter in a skillet until the vegetables are tender. Combine the chicken, onion mixture, shrimp, mayonnaise, pumpernickel bread, white bread, 1 cup reserved cooking liquid, mustard, capers, Worcestershire sauce and curry powder in a bowl and mix well. Spoon into a 3-quart baking dish. Bake at 350 degrees for 30 to 40 minutes or until bubbly. (**NOTE:** *You may prepare the casserole up to two days in advance and refrigerate, covered, until ready to bake. You can shred bread by pulsing in a blender or food processor.)*

Jumpin' Jambalaya

Serves 6

1 pound smoked sausage, chopped
1/2 cup vegetable oil
2 onions, chopped
1 bunch green onions, chopped
1 large green bell pepper, chopped
1/2 cup chopped celery
6 garlic cloves, minced
2 bay leaves
1/2 teaspoon salt
Pinch of cayenne pepper
2 pounds peeled shrimp
1 pound chicken, cooked and chopped
2 (16-ounce) cans chopped tomatoes
1 (6-ounce) can tomato paste
1/2 lemon, cut into quarters
3 cups cooked long-grain rice

Brown the sausage in the hot oil in a large heavy saucepan. Add the onions, green onions, bell pepper, celery, garlic, bay leaves, salt and cayenne pepper and sauté for 3 to 4 minutes. Stir in the shrimp, chicken, undrained tomatoes, tomato paste and lemon. Simmer until the shrimp turn pink, stirring frequently with a fork. Discard the bay leaves and lemon. Stir in the rice.

Alabama Seafood Gumbo

SERVES 6 TO 8

1 (28-ounce) can peeled tomatoes
3 tablespoons all-purpose flour
2 tablespoons bacon drippings
8 cups chicken broth
3 slices bacon
3 cups chopped okra
2 large onions, finely chopped
1 small green bell pepper, finely chopped
2 garlic cloves, crushed
4 bay leaves
1 teaspoon salt, or to taste
1 teaspoon black pepper
Dash of cayenne pepper
Dash of Worcestershire sauce
Dash of hot red pepper sauce
2 pounds shrimp
1 pint oysters, drained
1 pound crab meat, or meat picked from 6 cooked crabs
Hot cooked rice

Drain the tomatoes, reserving the juice. Combine the flour and bacon drippings in a medium saucepan over low heat and blend until smooth. Cook until the roux browns. Stir in the broth gradually and cook until thickened. Remove from the heat and set aside. Cook the bacon in a large heavy saucepan or stockpot until cooked through and crisp. Drain the bacon, reserving the bacon drippings in the pan. Sauté the okra, onions, bell pepper, garlic and tomatoes in the reserved bacon drippings until the onions are golden brown. Stir in the roux, reserved tomato juice, bay leaves, salt, black pepper, cayenne pepper, Worcestershire sauce and hot sauce. Simmer for 1 1/2 hours. Stir in the shrimp, oysters and crab meat. Simmer for 30 minutes. Taste and adjust the seasonings. Discard the bay leaves. Serve hot over rice. (**NOTE:** *The color of the gumbo will darken when the seafood is added.)*

After Hurricane Frederic devastated the Alabama Gulf Coast in 1979 and our home was completely destroyed, things were never quite the same when it came to gumbo. Of all the treasured family belongings lost, the most revered and lamented was the cast-iron gumbo pot, which was used for no other purpose. According to my mother, this family heirloom that had been seasoned and nurtured for a lifetime could never be replaced or re-created. The time-honored ritual of making gumbo continues, but the results are never quite as good as they would have been in "the" gumbo pot.

Seafood Royale

SERVES 8 TO 10

2 (10-ounce) cans cream of shrimp soup
1/2 cup mayonnaise
1 small onion, grated
1/4 cup (or more) cream, or 3/4 cup (or more) milk
Salt and white pepper to taste
Seasoned salt to taste
Nutmeg to taste
Cayenne pepper to taste
2 pounds cooked shrimp, peeled
3 cups cooked rice
1 (7-ounce) can crab meat, drained and flaked
1 1/2 cups chopped celery
1 (8-ounce) can water chestnuts, drained and chopped
3 tablespoons parsley
Paprika
Slivered almonds

Combine the soup and mayonnaise in a bowl and blend until smooth. Stir in the onion. Add the cream and mix well. Season with salt, white pepper, seasoned salt, nutmeg and cayenne pepper. Fold in the shrimp, rice, crab meat, celery, water chestnuts and parsley, adding additional cream if the mixture seems dry. Taste and adjust the seasonings. Spoon into a large buttered baking dish. Sprinkle generously with paprika and almonds. Bake at 350 degrees for 20 to 30 minutes or until heated through and bubbly. (**NOTE:** *This casserole freezes well.)*

Catfish Croquettes

SERVES 8

3 pounds catfish nuggets or fillets
1 cup dry plain bread crumbs
3/4 cup finely chopped celery
1/2 cup finely chopped onion
1/4 cup sour cream
3 eggs, lightly beaten
1 tablespoon lemon juice
1 teaspoon salt
1 teaspoon pepper
White cornmeal
Vegetable oil for frying

Steam the fish until flaky. Flake the fish with a fork or pulse in a food processor until flaked. Combine the fish, bread crumbs, celery, onion, sour cream, eggs, lemon juice, salt and pepper in a bowl and mix well. Shape into croquettes 1/2 cup at a time. Dredge in the cornmeal, shaking off any excess. Fry in hot oil in a deep heavy skillet until brown on each side. Drain on paper towels. Serve with tartar sauce or cocktail sauce on the side.

Catfish in the Coosa River have been documented to be over six feet long. Current fishermen often catch fish in the fifty- to seventy-five-pound range.

Artist Kelly Fitzpatrick (1888–1953) was a favorite son of Wetumpka, and owning a "Kelly" is better than being born rich. Kelly's vibrant and light-filled depictions of rural Alabama in the 1930s and '40s are distinctive and adored works. His famed Dixie Art Colony was on the banks of the Coosa.

Coosa Fish Camp Stew

SERVES 8

5 (14-ounce) cans diced tomatoes
1 (10-ounce) can diced tomatoes with green chiles
1 (12-ounce) can tomato paste
2 large onions, chopped
3 bell peppers, chopped
6 garlic cloves, crushed
1 cup dry white wine
1/2 cup olive oil
1/4 cup chopped fresh parsley
2 teaspoons Old Bay seasoning
1 bay leaf
2 pounds catfish fillets
Butter to taste
8 (1-inch-thick) slices French bread, toasted

Mix the tomatoes, tomatoes with green chiles, tomato paste, onions, bell peppers, garlic, wine, olive oil, parsley, Old Bay seasoning and bay leaf in a large saucepan. Bring to a boil and reduce the heat. Simmer for 2 to 3 hours, stirring occasionally. Steam the catfish until flaky. Discard the skin and bones. Add the fish and simmer for 1 hour, stirring occasionally. Spread the butter on the bread and place one slice in each of eight soup bowls. Ladle the stew over the bread. (**NOTE:** *Don't be afraid of using six garlic cloves. The flavor is rich, but not too garlicky.)*

Honey Sesame Salmon Steaks

SERVES 2

1/4 cup honey
Juice of 1 lemon
1/4 teaspoon grated ginger
1/8 teaspoon dry mustard
2 salmon steaks
1/2 teaspoon grated lemon zest
Sesame seeds
Parsley

Combine the honey, lemon juice, ginger and dry mustard in a bowl and mix well. Arrange the salmon side by side in a buttered baking dish. Pour or brush the glaze over the salmon. Sprinkle with the lemon zest and sesame seeds. Cover with aluminum foil. Bake at 350 degrees for 15 minutes. Uncover and bake for an additional 10 minutes or until the fish is light brown and just beginning to flake. Garnish with parsley.

Pan-Fried Tilapia

SERVES 4 TO 6

4 to 6 fresh or frozen tilapia fillets
Salt and pepper to taste
3 tablespoons all-purpose flour
1/4 cup peanut oil
1/4 cup (1/2 stick) butter
Juice of 1 lemon or lime
1 tablespoon finely chopped fresh parsley

Season the fish with salt and pepper and dust lightly with the flour. Cook in the hot peanut oil in a deep heavy skillet for 2 to 3 minutes on each side or until cooked through and brown. Remove to a serving plate, discarding the pan drippings. Combine the butter, lemon juice and parsley in the skillet and whisk until well combined. Pour the sauce over the fish.

HOME GROWN

It has been told that when Mr. Oscar died Ms. Lula sat and talked to the neighbors as they gathered. Somebody asked, "Well, just how did it happen, Ms. Lula?" She dolefully replied, "Well, he come home for dinner and I sent him out to the garden to cut a head of cabbage and he fell over dead."

The neighbor replied, "Oh, Ms. Lula, what on earth did you do?"
"Well, she said, I had to open a can of beans."

That story may not be true, but it does prove a point. We are dead serious about our vegetables. From the first delicate lettuces and tiny red radishes to the last cherished tomatoes picked before the first frost, we talk about and plan for how we're going to eat our vegetables.

There's no longer a garden in every backyard as there once was, but it is a rare yard that doesn't have a tomato vine or two, a few cucumbers, and some pepper plants, at least. Two or three zucchini plants can, and often do, feed a neighborhood. In fact, some people lock their car doors at night to keep their neighbors from putting a basket of zucchini in their back seat under the cover of darkness. Sharing the bounty of "a mess of beans" or a few ears of sweet corn is a way of life.

This section was generously sponsored by

BRANDT WRIGHT CENTURY 21 REALTY

Vegetables and Side Dishes

IT'S DIFFICULT

TO THINK ANYTHING

BUT PLEASANT THOUGHTS

WHILE EATING A

HOMEGROWN TOMATO.

LEWIS GRIZZARD

Vegetables

As the cookbook committee started collecting recipes, they sought traditional southern vegetable recipes from long-time southern cooks who typically remarked, "Why, honey, I cook vegetables the way my mamma and grandmamma did." So the committee began to ask these ladies to explain how their mammas and grandmammas cooked vegetables. These recipes are the result of the committee's quest for cooking vegetables southern style.

BUTTERBEANS

Choose small, young beans for boiling. Cover beans with water in a saucepan. Add 1 teaspoon bacon drippings, salt and pepper. Traditionally, fatback (streak-of-lean) was also added to the pan. Today's cooks tend to eschew the additional saturated fats, but the best flavor for peas, beans, greens and okra is achieved with bacon drippings.

OKRA

Boiled Okra: Trim most of the stem ends from young tender okra pods. Place in a saucepan and just barely cover with cold water. Add salt, pepper and bacon grease. Cook until tender. Overcooking will result in a slimy consistency.

Fried Okra: Cut tender okra pods into 1/2-inch slices. Place some cornmeal, a little flour and salt in a sealable plastic bag. Add the okra and shake. Place the okra in a strainer and shake off any excess cornmeal mixture. Fry in 350-degree oil, preferably peanut oil, until golden brown. Drain on paper towels and serve immediately.

PEAS

There is a large variety of peas available in the farmers' markets of the south during the summer months. Each of these varieties will require a different cooking time; therefore, the wise cook will taste the peas while cooking and cook them until just tender. They should be cooked using the same method used for butterbeans. Customarily peas were served with onions, pepper sauce and canned relishes such as chow-chow.

SWEET POTATOES

Scrub the sweet potatoes with a vegetable brush and dry well. Lightly oil the sweet potatoes and arrange in a baking dish. Bake at 375 degrees until soft. The time will depend on the size of the sweet potatoes. Leftover baked sweet potatoes may be peeled, cut into 1-inch slices and browned in butter in a skillet or mashed and used to make biscuits.

TURNIPS

Wash the greens thoroughly. Strip the leaves from any stems that are large. Bring 2 inches of water to a boil in a large saucepan or stockpot. Add the greens in two or three batches. The greens will reduce in volume as they wilt. Add a piece of fatback or a ham hock along with a couple tablespoons of bacon drippings and a couple teaspoons of salt. Cook until the greens are tender and are a deep dark green color. Serve with pepper sauce. The "pot likker" is delicious with corn bread crumbled into it.

Marinated Asparagus

Serves 8 to 10

2 pounds asparagus
Grated zest and juice of 1 large orange or 2 small oranges
5 large or 10 small fresh sage leaves
2 tablespoons raspberry wine vinegar or other red wine vinegar
1/4 teaspoon salt
1/2 cup olive oil
1/2 cup pistachios, coarsely chopped

Snap off the woody ends of the asparagus. Use a vegetable peeler to strip off the outer layer of each asparagus spear from just below the tip to the end of the spear. Steam the asparagus for 4 minutes or until tender-crisp. Let stand until cool. Dry well and place in a shallow baking dish. Process the orange zest, orange juice, sage, vinegar and salt in a food processor with a steel blade until combined and no solids are visible. Add the olive oil in a fine stream, processing constantly until incorporated. Pour over the asparagus, coating completely. Process the pistachios in a food processor until chopped. Spoon over the asparagus. Marinate, covered, in the refrigerator for 24 hours. (**Note:** *This dish is wonderful to serve as an appetizer or a side dish.)*

Asparagus with Radish Sauce

4 TO 6 SERVINGS

2 pounds asparagus
2 tablespoons olive oil
1/4 cup (1 ounce) grated Parmesan cheese
1/2 cup sliced green olives
1/4 cup finely chopped radishes
1/4 cup (1/2 stick) butter, melted
2 to 3 tablespoons lemon juice
2 tablespoons chopped green onions

Snap off the woody ends of the asparagus. Arrange the asparagus in a 3-quart rectangular baking dish. Drizzle with the olive oil and sprinkle with the cheese. Bake at 450 degrees for 15 minutes or until tender-crisp, tossing with tongs twice during baking. Place on a warm serving platter. Combine the olives, radishes, butter, lemon juice and green onions in a bowl and mix well. Pour over the asparagus.

Green Beans Delectable

SERVES 6 TO 8

2 (16-ounce) cans green beans
1 small onion, minced
Finely chopped garlic to taste
3 to 4 tablespoons bacon drippings
2 small tomatoes, peeled and chopped
3 to 4 tablespoons tarragon vinegar
1 tablespoon brown sugar
Salt and pepper to taste

Cook the green beans in a saucepan until heated through. Drain in a fine mesh strainer. Sauté the onion and garlic in the hot bacon drippings in the saucepan for 10 minutes. Add the tomatoes, vinegar, brown sugar, salt and pepper and sauté for 5 minutes. Stir in the green beans. Cook, covered, over low heat for 20 minutes. (**NOTE:** *This dish may be cooked ahead. To reheat, bake at 350 degrees in a casserole for 30 minutes.)*

Lemon Dill Green Beans

SERVES 4

3 tablespoons chopped fresh dill weed or 1 tablespoon dried dill weed
2 tablespoons olive oil
1 teaspoon salt
1 teaspoon grated lemon zest
1/3 cup fresh lemon juice
1 pound green beans
Crumbled feta cheese (optional)
Lemon slices
Fresh dill weed sprigs

Combine the dill weed, olive oil, salt, lemon zest and lemon juice in a large bowl and whisk well. Steam the green beans to the desired degree of crispness. Add the green beans to the dill mixture and toss gently to coat. Chill, covered, for 3 to 4 hours, tossing occasionally; drain. Arrange on a serving platter and sprinkle with feta cheese. Garnish with lemon slices and fresh dill weed sprigs.

Green Beans Dijon

SERVES 4 TO 6

1 pound green beans
Salt to taste
1/2 cup vegetable oil
1/2 cup tarragon vinegar
1 garlic clove, minced
1 tablespoon Dijon mustard
1 tablespoon dried parsley
1 teaspoon salt
1/8 teaspoon pepper

Rinse the green beans and remove the strings, leaving the green beans whole. Blanch the green beans in boiling salted water until tender-crisp; drain. Rinse the green beans under cold water until completely cool; drain. Dry the green beans and arrange in a shallow dish. Combine the oil, vinegar, garlic, Dijon mustard, parsley, salt and pepper in a jar with a tight-fitting lid and seal tightly. Shake to mix. Pour over the green beans and toss, coating completely. Serve immediately or marinate, covered, in the refrigerator for 8 to 10 hours before serving. (**NOTE:** *This dish keeps well in the refrigerator for 3 to 4 days.)*

Garbanzo Beans with Spinach and Sun-Dried Tomatoes

SERVES 2 TO 4

2 garlic cloves, minced
2 tablespoons olive oil
4 ounces spinach
1 (15-ounce) can garbanzo beans
1 1/2 teaspoons red wine vinegar
1/4 teaspoon salt
1/4 teaspoon red pepper flakes
1/4 cup sun-dried tomatoes, chopped
1/3 cup couscous, cooked
Crumbled feta cheese or grated Parmesan cheese

Sauté the garlic in the hot olive oil in a large skillet over medium heat until aromatic. Add the spinach and sauté until wilted. Add the garbanzo beans , vinegar, salt and red pepper flakes and mix well. Bring to a simmer and stir in the tomatoes. Spoon the garbanzo bean mixture over the couscous and sprinkle with cheese.

Broccoli with Olive Butter

SERVES 12

4 (12-ounce) packages frozen broccoli spears, cooked
1 teaspoon seasoned salt, or to taste
2 garlic cloves, crushed
2/3 cup butter, melted
12 large stuffed olives, sliced
4 teaspoons fresh lemon juice
1/2 teaspoon pepper

Arrange the broccoli on a warm serving platter and sprinkle with the seasoning salt. Sauté the garlic in the butter in a small saucepan over low heat for 15 minutes. Add the olives, lemon juice and pepper and cook until heated through; do not boil. Pour evenly over the broccoli. (**NOTE:** *You may substitute fresh broccoli for the frozen.)*

Brussels Sprouts and Artichoke Casserole

SERVES 6 TO 8

1 cup water
2 (10-ounce) packages frozen Brussels sprouts
28 ounces drained canned artichokes, cut into eights
1 to 1 1/3 cups mayonnaise
1/2 cup (1 stick) butter, cut into pieces and softened
1/2 cup (2 ounces) Parmesan cheese
1/2 cup sliced almonds
4 teaspoons lemon juice
1 teaspoon celery salt

Bring the water to a boil in a saucepan. Add the Brussels sprouts and cook until tender; drain. Arrange the Brussels sprouts and artichokes evenly in a greased baking dish. Combine the mayonnaise, butter, cheese, almonds, lemon juice and salt in a bowl and mix well. Spread over the vegetables. Bake at 350 degrees for 20 to 30 minutes or until brown and bubbly. (**NOTE:** *You may substitute fresh Brussels sprouts for the frozen.)*

Cabbage and Leeks in Cream Sauce

SERVES 8 TO 10

1/2 head cabbage, coarsely chopped
3 large leeks, sliced
2 tablespoons water, or 1/4 cup chicken broth
2 tablespoons sherry or dry white wine
1 large garlic clove, minced
3 tablespoons butter
2 tablespoons flour
3/4 to 1 cup milk or half-and-half
1/4 teaspoon mace or nutmeg
Salt and pepper to taste

Place the cabbage, leeks, water, sherry and garlic in a slow cooker. Dot with 1 tablespoon of the butter. Cook on Low for 7 to 9 hours. Melt the remaining 2 tablespoons butter in a saucepan. Stir in the flour. Cook until smooth and bubbly, stirring constantly. Add the milk gradually, stirring constantly until combined. Cook over low heat until thickened, stirring often. Add the mace, salt and pepper and mix well. Stir into the cabbage mixture. (**NOTE:** *You may cook the cabbage mixture in a skillet over low heat. This method will require additional water or broth.)*

Black-Eyed Peas with Tomato and Onion Sauce

SERVES 6

1 cup dried black-eyed peas, sorted and rinsed
4 cups cold water
1 onion, chopped
1/4 to 1/2 cup good-quality light olive oil
1/2 teaspoon crushed garlic
1 3/4 cups chopped seeded peeled tomatoes
1 teaspoon salt, or to taste
1/2 teaspoon pepper, or to taste
2 tablespoons finely chopped parsley

Combine the peas and water in a large saucepan. Cook over medium-high heat for 30 to 40 minutes or until tender but still firm; drain. (The peas should not have a raw taste.) Run under cold water until completely cool; drain. Sauté the onion in the hot olive oil for 1 minute. Add the garlic and tomatoes and simmer on low for 30 minutes, stirring often. Stir in the peas. Season with the salt and pepper. Cook for 10 minutes, stirring frequently. Add the parsley and mix well. Spoon into a baking dish and keep warm until ready to serve. (**NOTE:** *Dried black-eyed peas will cook at different rates. Check for doneness often and do not overcook. This dish may be reheated in the oven.)*

Field Pea Casserole

Serves 8

2 (15-ounce) cans field peas
3 large tomatoes, sliced
3 green bell peppers, cut into rings
3 large white onions, sliced
1/2 cup (2 ounces) grated Parmesan cheese
Cayenne pepper to taste
Salt to taste
6 slices bacon

Alternate layers of the field peas, tomatoes, bell peppers and onions in the order listed in a 9×13-inch baking dish until all of the ingredients are used. Sprinkle with the cheese, cayenne pepper and salt. Arrange the bacon slices over the top. Bake, covered with aluminum foil, at 400 degrees for 1 hour. Uncover and broil until the bacon is cooked through and crisp. Serve hot.

Onion Shortcake

Serves 8 to 10

2 cups buttermilk biscuit mix
2/3 cup milk
3 large onions, sliced
2 tablespoons butter, melted
2 eggs
1 (5-ounce) can evaporated milk
1/2 teaspoon salt
1/4 teaspoon pepper

Combine the biscuit mix and milk in a bowl and mix until a soft dough forms. Sauté the onions in the butter in a skillet until tender. Combine the eggs, evaporated milk, salt and pepper in a bowl and beat until smooth. Press the dough with floured hands into a greased 7×11-inch baking dish. Spread the onions evenly over the dough. Pour the egg mixture on top. Bake at 350 degrees for 30 minutes or until brown.

Shirley Eberhart's Country Company Potatoes

SERVES 8

6 or 7 potatoes
1/2 cup (1 stick) butter
1 (10-ounce) can cream of chicken soup
2 cups sour cream
1 1/2 cups (6 ounces) shredded Cheddar cheese
3 tablespoons grated onion
1 teaspoon salt
1/2 teaspoon pepper
2 cups cornflakes, crumbled
1/4 cup (1/2 stick) butter, melted

Combine the potatoes with cold water to cover in a large saucepan. Bring to a boil. Boil for 20 minutes; drain. Let stand until completely cool. Peel and grate the potatoes. Combine 1/2 cup butter and the soup in a saucepan. Cook until smooth and heated through, stirring often. Remove from the heat and stir in the sour cream, cheese, onion, salt and pepper. Fold in the potatoes. Spoon into a 9×13-inch baking dish. Combine the cereal and 1/4 melted butter in a bowl. Sprinkle over the potato mixture. Chill, covered, in the refrigerator for 8 to 10 hours. Bake, uncovered, at 350 degrees for 45 to 60 minutes or until heated through and brown. (**NOTE:** *Men love this dish. It takes little time to prepare, and because it must be made a day in advance, it makes a wonderful dish for dinner parties. You may freeze, covered, until baking time instead of refrigerating.)*

Rosemary Roasted Potatoes with Goat Cheese

SERVES 6

10 cups cubed yellow or baking potatoes (about 4 pounds)
6 garlic cloves, chopped
3 tablespoons balsamic vinegar
2 tablespoons chopped fresh rosemary, or 2 teaspoons dried rosemary
1 tablespoon olive oil
1/2 teaspoon salt
1/4 teaspoon pepper
3/4 cup crumbled goat cheese

Combine the potatoes, garlic, vinegar, rosemary, olive oil, salt and pepper in a sealable plastic bag. Seal and shake until well coated. Spoon onto a baking sheet sprayed with nonstick cooking spray. Bake at 400 degrees for 45 minutes or until brown. Spoon into a large serving bowl. Sprinkle with the cheese and toss well.

Rosemary Roasted Sweet Potatoes

SERVES 6 TO 8

4 pounds sweet potatoes, cut into 1/2-inch pieces
1/4 cup olive oil
2 to 3 tablespoons fresh rosemary leaves
4 teaspoons minced garlic
1/2 cup minced fresh parsley
1 teaspoon salt
1/2 teaspoon freshly ground pepper

Combine the sweet potatoes, olive oil, rosemary and garlic in a large bowl or sealable plastic bag and toss or shake until well coated. Spoon onto 1 or 2 rimmed baking sheets, spreading the sweet potatoes out in a single layer. Bake at 375 to 400 degrees for 15 to 30 minutes. Sprinkle with parsley, salt and pepper and toss well.

Sweet Potato Casserole

SERVES 10 TO 12

Sweet Potatoes

2 (29-ounce) cans cut sweet potatoes, or
4 cups mashed baked fresh sweet potatoes
1 cup packed light brown sugar
2 eggs, lightly beaten
1/3 cup butter, softened
1/3 cup milk
1 1/2 teaspoons vanilla extract

Topping

1 cup packed light brown sugar
1 cup chopped pecans
1/3 cup all-purpose flour
1/3 cup butter, melted

To prepare the sweet potatoes, bring the undrained sweet potatoes to a boil in a saucepan. Cook for 15 minutes or until tender. Remove from the heat and drain. Beat in a mixing bowl until mashed. Add the brown sugar, eggs, butter, milk and vanilla and mix well. Spread evenly into a buttered 2-quart baking dish.

To prepare the topping, combine the brown sugar, pecans, flour and butter in a bowl and mix until crumbly. Sprinkle evenly over the sweet potato mixture. Bake at 350 degrees for 30 to 35 minutes or until a knife inserted near the center comes out clean. (**NOTE:** *You may substitute marshmallows for the pecan topping. Cover the sweet potato mixture with marshmallows during the last 10 minutes of baking.)*

Summer Squash Casserole

SERVES 6

1 pound yellow squash, chopped
1 onion, chopped
1/2 cup French-fried onions
1/2 cup (2 ounces) shredded sharp Cheddar cheese
1/4 cup (1/2 stick) butter, softened
1 egg, lightly beaten
1 tablespoon (heaping) sour cream
1 teaspoon salt
1/2 sleeve round crackers, crushed
1/4 cup (1/2 stick) butter, melted

Bring a small amount of water to a boil in a saucepan. Add the squash and onion and cook until tender. Drain well and mash. Place in a bowl and stir in the French-fried onions, cheese, 1/4 cup butter, the egg, sour cream and salt. Spoon into a greased baking dish. Bake at 375 degrees for 30 minutes. Sprinkle with the crackers and drizzle with 1/4 cup melted butter. Bake until brown.

Red Eagle, a name seen frequently in our area, is the name used for William Weatherford, an outstanding leader and warrior among the Creeks.

Turnip Green Casserole

Serves 6 to 8

1 (15-ounce) can turnip greens, partially drained
1/2 (10-ounce) can cream of mushroom soup
1/2 cup mayonnaise
2 eggs, lightly beaten
1 tablespoon apple cider vinegar
1 teaspoon horseradish
Salt and pepper to taste
1/2 cup (2 ounces) shredded sharp Cheddar cheese
1/2 cup cracker crumbs

Mix the turnip greens, soup, mayonnaise, eggs, vinegar and horseradish in a bowl. Season with salt and pepper. Spoon into a greased 8×8-inch baking dish. Bake at 350 degrees for 45 to 55 minutes or until firm. Sprinkle with the cheese and top with the cracker crumbs. Bake for 10 minutes or until the cheese melts and the cracker crumbs brown. (**Note:** *You may use cream of chicken soup for the cream of mushroom soup. This recipe may be doubled and baked in a 9×13-inch baking dish.)*

Green Tomato and Vidalia Onion Tart

SERVES 6 TO 8

1 (9-inch) deep dish pie shell
1 large Vidalia onion, thinly sliced
1 tablespoon olive oil
2 green tomatoes, thinly sliced
2 tablespoons chopped chives
1/2 teaspoon dried basil
1/2 teaspoon sugar
1/4 teaspoon salt
1/4 teaspoon pepper
1/2 cup mayonnaise
1/2 cup (2 ounces) shredded sharp Cheddar cheese
1 teaspoon lemon juice

Bake the pie shell according to the package directions. Sauté the onion in the hot olive oil in a skillet just until tender. Spread the onion in the pie shell. Top with the tomatoes. Sprinkle evenly with the chives, basil, sugar, salt and pepper. Combine the mayonnaise, cheese and lemon juice in a bowl and mix well. Spread evenly over the prepared layers. Bake at 375 degrees on a baking sheet for 30 minutes or until golden brown and bubbly. (**NOTE:** *You may use biscuit dough for making the crust instead of a pie shell. A biscuit crust holds together better than the pie crust.*

Tomato Pie

SERVES 6 TO 8

1 refrigerator pie pastry
4 large tomatoes, peeled and sliced
1/2 teaspoon salt
1/4 teaspoon pepper
1/4 cup mashed roasted garlic (see note below)
1 1/2 cups (6 ounces) shredded fontina cheese

Unfold the pastry into a pie plate. Fit the pastry into the plate and trim the edge. Bake at 450 degrees for 9 minutes or until the pastry is light brown. Let stand until cool. Sprinkle the tomato slices evenly with the salt and pepper and place on folded paper towels. Let stand for 10 minutes or until the paper towels absorb most of the tomato juice. Spread the roasted garlic in the bottom of the pie shell. Layer with 1/2 cup of the cheese and the tomato slices. Top with the remaining 1 cup cheese. Bake at 350 degrees for 30 minutes or until the cheese is melted and light brown. (**NOTE:** *To prepare roasted garlic, cut off the tops of three garlic bulbs and place cut side up on a baking sheet lined with aluminum foil. Drizzle with olive oil. Bake at 350 degrees for 2 hours or until the garlic is brown and fragrant. Remove from the oven and let stand until completely cool. Squeeze the bulbs from the base, releasing the garlic pulp into a container with a lid. Store in the refrigerator and use as needed.)*

Baked Tomato Slices

SERVES 6

3 tomatoes, cut into 1/2-inch slices
1/4 cup chopped or thinly sliced onion
2 tablespoons melted butter or olive oil
1/2 teaspoon dried basil
1/8 teaspoon pepper

Layer the tomatoes and onion in a glass baking dish. Drizzle with the butter and sprinkle with the basil and pepper. Bake at 350 degrees for 15 to 20 minutes or until heated through. (**NOTE:** *This dish may be prepared in advance and refrigerated until ready to serve.)*

Zucchini Pasta Bake

SERVE 6

8 ounces penne
Salt to taste
1/2 cup crushed saltine crackers
1/4 cup (1 ounce) grated Parmesan cheese
1/2 onion, chopped
1 tablespoon olive oil
2 cups chopped zucchini
1 tomato, chopped
2 garlic cloves, minced
1/2 teaspoon dried oregano
1/2 teaspoon dried basil
1 pinch celery seeds
Pepper to taste
1 cup (4 ounces) shredded mozzarella cheese

Cook the pasta in boiling salted water in a saucepan for 10 to 12 minutes or until al dente; drain. Process the crackers and Parmesan cheese in a blender or food processor until combined. Sauté the onion in the hot olive oil in a large skillet over medium heat until tender. Add the zucchini, tomato, garlic, oregano, basil and celery seeds. Season with salt and pepper. Sauté until the zucchini is tender. Remove from the heat and fold in the pasta and mozzarella cheese. Spoon into a lightly greased baking dish. Sprinkle evenly with the cracker mixture. Bake at 350 degrees for 25 minutes or until the top is light brown. Let stand for 5 minutes.

When Beulah Farmer started a little political straw poll of regulars who gathered at Twin Pines Grocery in Slapout, little did she expect that one day she'd be receiving calls from The Washington Post *and* The New York Times. *Her poll of Beat 14 voters had uncanny success in predicting state and national elections for years. In addition to being a famous pollster, Beulah was renowned for the corn bread dressing she served for Thanksgiving and Christmas.*

Mama's Dressing

SERVES 12

1 large pan hot buttermilk corn bread
Butter, softened
4 cups chicken broth
6 eggs
1 (12-ounce) can evaporated milk
3 cups cooked white rice
1 large yellow onion, chopped
1 cup chopped celery
1/2 cup (1 stick) butter, melted
Sage to taste
Pepper to taste

Brush the corn bread with softened butter. Let stand until completely cool. Crumble into a large bowl. Combine the broth, eggs and evaporated milk in a bowl and mix well. Pour over the corn bread and mix well. Stir in the rice, onion, celery and 1/2 cup melted butter. Season with sage and pepper. Spoon into a large greased baking dish and cook at 450 degrees for 50 to 60 minutes.

Macaroni and Cheese Deluxe

SERVES 6 TO 8

8 ounces elbow macaroni
2 cups cream-style cottage cheese
2 cups (8 ounces) shredded sharp Cheddar cheese
1 cup sour cream
1 egg, lightly beaten
3/4 teaspoon salt
Dash of pepper
Paprika

Cook the pasta according to the package directions. Rinse with cold water; drain and set aside. Combine the cottage cheese, Cheddar cheese, sour cream, egg, salt and pepper in a bowl and mix well. Fold in the pasta. Spoon into a greased 2-quart baking dish. Sprinkle with paprika. Bake at 350 degrees for 45 minutes.

Hot Buttered Pineapple

SERVES 4 TO 6

1/4 cup (1/2 stick) butter
1/4 cup packed dark brown sugar
1/4 cup dark rum
1 pineapple, cored and cut into bite-size pieces
Toasted shredded coconut
Ground allspice

Cook the butter, brown sugar and rum in a skillet over low heat until thick and bubbly, stirring occasionally. Stir in the pineapple, coating completely. Cook until heated through. Divide among four to six bowls and spoon the remaining syrup over each serving. Garnish with coconut and allspice.

FLOUR SACK MASTERPIECES

Before the days of Duncan Hines, Blue Bell, and Sara Lee, everybody made desserts . . . most from combinations of readily available ingredients: sugar, milk, butter, flour, and eggs. Combinations of these basic ingredients produced the time-honored desserts of the South, such as tea cakes, pound cakes, jelly rolls, banana puddings, and fruit pies. More elaborate desserts were reserved for the holidays when citrus fruits, candied fruits, and coconuts could be found in the local grocery, and pecans were available from your yard or your neighbor's. Fruitcakes were made weeks ahead of Christmas and wrapped in a clean flour sack soaked in wine or whiskey. Lane Cakes and ambrosia were as much a part of Christmas as a cedar tree.

Homemade ice cream was a favorite special treat. "Come by this evening; we're gonna churn some ice cream," brought family and neighbors without fail. No special occasion like the Fourth of July, family reunions, or church homecomings was complete without this labor of love, and many will remember sitting on newspapers on top of the freezer while the ice cream churned.

We continue the tradition of gathering to celebrate special occasions. One of our notable celebrations is Christmas on the Coosa, which occurs in early December and welcomes Christmas as only a river town can. The parade, arts and crafts vendors, and a flotilla of elaborately decorated boats for the Boat Parade are perfect accompaniments for what we consider the main event—Trinity's sale of Bessie Brand's Camp Stew.

Summer brings the bounty of orchards and you-pick-it farms. Local strawberries, blueberries, blackberries, famous peaches from neighboring Chilton County, pears, and fall's muscadines and scuppernongs provide months of delectable cobblers and pies.

This section was generously sponsored by

PRIME SOUTH BANK

ALL'S WELL

THAT

ENDS WELL.

SHAKESPEARE

Episcopalian Cake

SERVES 10 TO 12

Cake

3 cups all-purpose flour
1 teaspoon baking powder
1/4 teaspoon each baking soda and salt
1 cup (2 sticks) unsalted butter, softened
2 cups sugar
4 eggs, at room temperature
1 tablespoon grated orange zest
1 tablespoon orange-flavored liqueur
1 1/2 teaspoons vanilla extract
1 cup plain yogurt
Orange Whipped Cream Frosting (page 151)

Fillings

1 cup fresh orange juice
1/4 cup orange-flavored liqueur
1/4 cup sugar
1 1/3 cups orange marmalade

To prepare the cake, sift the flour, baking powder, baking soda and salt together. Beat the butter in a mixing bowl until smooth. Add the sugar gradually, beating until light and fluffy. Beat in the eggs one at a time. Beat in the orange zest, liqueur and vanilla. Add the flour mixture and yogurt alternately, mixing well after each addition and ending with the flour mixture. Spoon into three 9-inch cake pans sprayed with nonstick cooking spray. Smooth the surfaces and tap the pans on the counter to release any air pockets. Bake at 325 degrees for 30 to 35 minutes or until the layers test done. Cool in the pans on a wire rack for 20 minutes.

To prepare the fillings, mix the orange juice, liqueur and sugar in a bowl, stirring until the sugar dissolves. Spoon over the cake in the pans. Let stand until the layers are cool and the syrup has been absorbed. Remove the cake layers to a wire rack. Microwave the marmalade in a microwave-safe bowl on High for 30 seconds or until melted. Let stand for 5 minutes.

To assemble, arrange one cake layer on a serving plate. Spread 1/2 cup of the marmalade over the layer. Invert a second cake on top. Spread 1/2 cup of the marmalade over the cake layer. Invert the remaining cake on top. Spread the remaining 1/3 cup marmalade over the top, leaving a 1 1/4-inch border around the edge. Spread the frosting over the side and the exposed border on the top. Chill, covered, until ready to serve.

Orange Whipped Cream Frosting

MAKES 4 CUPS

2 cups heavy whipping cream, chilled
1/4 cup confectioners' sugar
1 tablespoon orange-flavored liqueur

Beat the cream, confectioners' sugar and liqueur in a bowl until stiff peaks form.

Espresso Chocolate Torte

SERVES 12 TO 16

2 1/2 cups (5 sticks) unsalted butter, cut into pieces
2 1/4 cups sugar
3 cups (18 ounces) semisweet chocolate chips
1 cup plus 2 tablespoons strong brewed coffee
1/4 teaspoon vanilla extract
9 eggs, beaten
Whipped cream

Combine the butter, sugar, chocolate chips, coffee and vanilla in a 3-quart saucepan. Cook until the chocolate is melted and the mixture is very hot, stirring constantly. Add to the eggs gradually, beating constantly until combined. Pour into a large greased springform pan.

Bake at 250 degrees for 2 hours. Refrigerate, covered, until the cake is set. Remove the side of the springform pan. Let stand until room temperature. Serve with whipped cream.

Jeanette Belcher's Creole Cake

Serves 15

Cake

2 eggs
2 cups sugar
1/2 cup vegetable oil
2 tablespoons baking cocoa
1/2 cup buttermilk
1 teaspoon baking soda
1/2 teaspoon vanilla extract
2 cups all-purpose flour
1 cup boiling water

Coconut Pecan Topping

1/2 cup (1 stick) butter, melted
1 (1-pound) package brown sugar
1 (3-ounce) can flaked coconut
1 cup pecans, chopped
1 (5-ounce) can evaporated milk
1 teaspoon vanilla extract

To prepare the cake, combine the eggs and sugar in a large bowl and blend until smooth. Add the vegetable oil, baking cocoa, buttermilk, baking soda, vanilla, flour and boiling water in the order listed, mixing well after each addition. Pour into a 11×16-inch cake pan. Bake at 350 degrees for 30 to 45 minutes or until the cake tests done.

To prepare the topping, mix the butter, brown sugar, coconut, pecans, evaporated milk and vanilla in a bowl. Spread evenly over the hot cake. Place on the highest oven rack and broil until bubbly.

Bette's Chocolate Sheet Cake

SERVES 15

Cake

2 cups all-purpose flour
2 cups sugar
1/4 teaspoon salt
1/2 cup (1 stick) butter
1/2 cup shortening, or 1/2 cup (1 stick) unsalted butter
1/4 cup baking cocoa
1 cup water
1/2 cup buttermilk
1 teaspoon baking soda
1 teaspoon cinnamon (optional)
2 eggs, lightly beaten
1 teaspoon vanilla extract

Chocolate Pecan Icing

1/2 cup (1 stick) butter
6 tablespoons milk
1/4 cup baking cocoa
1 (1-pound) package confectioners' sugar, sifted
1 cup chopped pecans
1 teaspoon vanilla extract

To prepare the cake, sift the flour, sugar and salt into a medium bowl; set aside. Place the butter, shortening, baking cocoa and water in a saucepan. Bring to a rapid boil, stirring constantly. Pour over the flour mixture and stir well by hand. Add the buttermilk, baking soda, cinnamon, eggs and vanilla in the order listed, mixing well after each addition. Pour into a greased 11×16-inch baking pan. Bake at 400 degrees for 20 minutes. (**NOTE:** *The cake may be baked in two small greased pans.)*

To prepare the icing, combine the butter, milk, and baking cocoa in a saucepan. Bring to a rapid boil, stirring constantly. Remove from the heat and stir in the confectioners' sugar, pecans and vanilla. Spread over the hot cake. (**NOTE:** *Begin the icing about 5 minutes before the cake is finished baking.)*

Apple Spice Cake

SERVES 12

Cake

3 cups all-purpose flour
1 tablespoon cinnamon
1 teaspoon baking soda
1 teaspoon salt
2 cups sugar
1 1/3 cups vegetable oil
3 eggs
1 teaspoon vanilla extract
3 or 4 Granny Smith apples, cored and cut into 1/2-inch pieces
1 cup chopped pecans or walnuts (optional)

Caramel Sauce

1 cup packed light brown sugar
1/2 cup (1 stick) unsalted butter
1/4 cup evaporated milk
1 teaspoon vanilla extract
Pinch of salt (optional)

To prepare the cake, sift the flour, cinnamon, baking soda and salt together. Beat the sugar, oil, eggs and vanilla in a mixing bowl until smooth. Add the dry ingredients gradually, beating constantly until combined. Fold in the apples and pecans. Pour the batter into a greased and floured 12-cup bundt pan. Bake at 350 degrees for 1 1/4 to 1 1/2 hours or until the cake tests done. Cool slightly in the pan on a wire rack. Remove to a wire rack to cool completely. Drizzle the caramel sauce over the cake just before serving.

To prepare the sauce, combine the brown sugar, butter, evaporated milk, vanilla and salt in a saucepan over medium heat. Cook until thickened, stirring constantly. Be careful not to burn the sauce.

Orange Date Nut Cake

SERVES 16

1/2 cup (1 stick) butter, softened
1 cup sugar
2 eggs
2 tablespoons grated orange zest
2 cups all-purpose flour
1 teaspoon baking soda
2/3 cup buttermilk
1 cup dates, chopped
1/2 cup pecans, chopped
1/4 cup all-purpose flour
Juice of 2 oranges
1/2 cup sugar

Cream the butter and 1 cup sugar in a mixing bowl until light and fluffy. Add the eggs and beat until fluffy. Add the orange zest and mix well. Sift 2 cups flour and the baking soda together. Add the dry ingredients and buttermilk alternately to the creamed mixture, mixing well after each addition and ending with dry ingredients. Combine the dates, pecans and 1/4 cup flour in a bowl and toss to coat. Fold into the batter. Pour the batter into a greased and floured tube pan. Bake at 350 degrees for 40 to 45 minutes or until the cake tests done. Combine the orange juice and 1/2 cup sugar in a bowl. Stir until the sugar is dissolved. Pour over the cake and let stand to cool completely in the tube pan.

Pineapple Cake

SERVES 24

3 cups all-purpose flour
1 teaspoon baking powder
1 cup (2 sticks) salted butter, softened
1/2 cup shortening
2 3/4 cups sugar
6 eggs
1/4 cup milk
1 teaspoon vanilla extract
8 ounces crushed pineapple

Combine the flour and baking powder and mix well. Beat the butter and shortening in a mixing bowl until smooth. Add the sugar gradually, beating until light and fluffy. Add the eggs one at a time, mixing well after each addition. Add the flour mixture alternately with the milk, blending well after each addition and ending with the flour mixture. Stir in the vanilla and pineapple. Pour into two greased loaf pans. Bake at 325 degrees for 1 hour to 1 1/4 hours or until the loaves test done. Lower the temperature to 300 degrees if the cakes begin to brown too soon. Cool completely. Wrap in plastic wrap and store at room temperature for 3 days before serving. (**NOTE:** *For sweeter cakes, drizzle with pineapple juice and dust with confectioners' sugar before serving.)*

White Fruitcake

SERVES 16

4 cups pecans, chopped
16 ounces candied pineapple, chopped
12 ounces candied cherries, chopped
1 3/4 cups all-purpose flour
1/2 teaspoon baking powder
1 cup (2 sticks) butter, softened
1 cup sugar
5 eggs, beaten
1/2 cup applesauce
1 tablespoon vanilla extract
1 tablespoon lemon extract (optional)

Line a greased 10-inch tube pan with greased baking parchment. Combine the pecans, pineapple, cherries and 1/4 cup of the flour in a bowl and toss to coat; set aside. Sift the remaining 1 1/2 cups flour and the baking powder together. Beat the butter and sugar in a mixing bowl until light and fluffy. Add the eggs and beat until smooth. Fold in the dry ingredients and applesauce alternately, mixing well after each addition. Fold in the pecan mixture, vanilla and lemon extract. Pour the batter into the prepared pan. Place in a cold oven and bake at 250 degrees for 3 hours. Cool completely in the pan on a wire rack.

For Medicinal Purposes Only
In many southern homes, alcoholic drinks were not allowed, but whiskey could be used for soaking fruitcakes or to relieve a cough or sore throat. Colds seemed to come on with amazing frequency. Homemade blackberry and muscadine wine might also be enjoyed on rare occasions, as long as the preacher wasn't visiting.

Lane Cake

SERVES 18

Cake

1 cup (2 sticks) butter or margarine, softened
2 cups sugar
1 teaspoon vanilla extract
3 1/4 cups sifted all-purpose flour
1 tablespoon baking powder
3/4 teaspoon salt
1 cup milk
8 egg whites, at room temperature

Lane Frosting

12 egg yolks
1 3/4 cups sugar
3/4 cup (1 1/2 sticks) butter or margarine, softened
1/2 teaspoon salt
1/2 to 3/4 cup bourbon
1 1/2 cups pecans, chopped
1 1/2 cups golden raisins, chopped
1 1/2 cups flaked fresh coconut or frozen flaked coconut
1/2 cup candied cherries, cut into quarters (optional)

To prepare the cake, grease three 9-inch cake pans and line with baking parchment. Beat the butter in a mixing bowl until smooth. Beat in the sugar gradually until light and fluffy. Beat in the vanilla and mix well. Combine the flour, baking powder and salt. Add to the creamed mixture alternately with the milk, mixing well after each addition. Beat the egg whites in a mixing bowl until firm peaks form and fold into the batter. Spoon evenly into the prepared pans. Bake at 350 degrees for 18 to 20 minutes or until the layers test done. Cool in the pans for 10 minutes. Remove to a wire rack to cool completely.

To prepare the frosting, combine the egg yolks, sugar, butter and salt in the top of a double boiler. Beat with a hand mixer for 30 seconds or until blended. Place the egg yolk mixture over boiling water. Reduce the heat to low and cook for 20 minutes or until the mixture is slightly thickened, stirring constantly. Remove from the heat. Add the bourbon and beat at low speed for 1 minute. Combine the pecans, raisins, coconut and cherries in a bowl and mix well. Pour the egg yolk mixture over the top and stir well. Let stand until completely cool.

To assemble the cake, slice each cake into halves horizontally, making six layers. Spread the frosting between the layers and over the top and side of the cake. Refrigerate, covered, for two weeks before serving. (**NOTE:** *To mellow the cake, you may brush a small amount of bourbon on the top of each layer before spreading the frosting.)*

Pumpkin Crunch Cake

SERVES 18 TO 20

1 (29-ounce) can pumpkin
1 (12-ounce) can evaporated milk
1 cup sugar
4 eggs
2 teaspoons cinnamon
1 teaspoon ginger
1 teaspoon vanilla extract
1/2 teaspoon nutmeg
1/4 teaspoon ground cloves
1/8 teaspoon salt
1 (2-layer) package yellow cake mix
1 cup chopped pecans
1 cup (2 sticks) unsalted butter, melted

Combine the pumpkin, evaporated milk, sugar and eggs in a bowl and mix until combined. Stir in the cinnamon, ginger, vanilla, nutmeg, cloves and salt. Pour into a greased 9×13-inch baking pan. Sprinkle evenly with the cake mix and pecans. Drizzle the butter evenly over the top. Bake at 350 degrees for 1 hour.

Pumpkin Roll

SERVES 8 TO 12

1 cup granulated sugar
3/4 cup all-purpose flour
2/3 cup puréed pumpkin
3 eggs
1 teaspoon baking soda
1 teaspoon cinnamon
8 ounces cream cheese, softened
1/4 cup (1/2 stick) butter, softened
1 cup confectioners' sugar
1/2 teaspoon vanilla extract
Chopped pecans (optional)

Mix the granulated sugar, flour, pumpkin, eggs, baking soda and cinnamon in a bowl until combined. Pour into a greased and floured 10×15-inch cake pan. Bake at 375 degrees for 15 minutes or until the cake tests done. Invert the cake onto a clean kitchen towel. Roll the warm cake in the towel as for a jelly roll and place on a wire rack to cool. Unroll the cooled cake carefully and remove the towel. Combine the cream cheese, butter and confectioners' sugar in a bowl and mix until combined. Stir in the vanilla and pecans. Spread to the edges of the cake and reroll. Place seam side down on a serving plate.

Katyleene Kendall's Gingerbread with Lemon Sauce

SERVES 6 TO 8

Gingerbread
2/3 cup shortening
1/4 cup sugar
3/4 cup molasses
2 cups sifted all-purpose flour
1 1/4 teaspoons baking powder
1 teaspoon ginger
3/4 teaspoon salt
1/2 teaspoon baking soda
2 eggs, beaten
1/2 cup milk

Lemon Sauce
1 cup sugar
1/2 cup (1 stick) butter
1/4 cup water
1 egg, beaten
Grated zest of 1 lemon
1/4 cup lemon juice

To prepare the gingerbread, cream the shortening and sugar in a mixing bowl until light and fluffy. Add the molasses gradually, beating until incorporated. Sift the flour, baking powder, ginger, salt and baking soda together. Add half the dry ingredients to the molasses mixture and beat until combined. Add the eggs and mix well. Add the remaining dry ingredients alternately with the milk, beating well after each addition. Pour into a greased and floured 8-inch baking pan. Bake at 325 degrees for 1 hour or until the gingerbread tests done.

To prepare the sauce, combine the sugar, butter, water, egg, lemon zest and lemon juice in a saucepan. Cook over medium heat until the sauce comes to a boil, stirring constantly. Serve warm spooned over the gingerbread. (**NOTE:** *The lemon sauce may be stored in the refrigerator. Warm in the microwave as needed.)*

Brown Sugar Pound Cake

SERVES 16

Cake

1 cup (2 sticks) butter or margarine, softened
1/2 cup shortening
1 (1-pound) package light brown sugar
1/2 cup granulated sugar
5 eggs
3 cups all-purpose flour
1/2 teaspoon baking powder
1 cup milk
1 cup chopped pecans
2 tablespoons vanilla extract

Cream Cheese Frosting

1/2 cup butter (1 stick) butter or margarine, softened
8 ounces cream cheese, softened
1 (1-pound) package confectioners' sugar
2 teaspoons vanilla extract

To prepare the cake, cream the butter and shortening in a mixing bowl. Add the brown sugar and granulated sugar gradually, beating constantly until light and fluffy. Add the eggs one at a time, mixing well after each addition. Combine the flour and baking powder and mix well. Add to the sugar mixture alternately with the milk, mixing well after each addition and ending with the dry ingredients. Add the pecans and vanilla and mix well. Pour into a greased and floured 10-inch tube pan. Bake at 350 degrees for 1 hour and 10 minutes or until the cake tests done. Cool in the pan for 10 minutes. Remove to a wire rack to cool completely.

To prepare the frosting, cream the butter and cream cheese in a mixing bowl. Add the powdered sugar and vanilla and beat until combined. Frost the cooled cake.

Whipping Cream Pound Cake

SERVES 16

1 cup (2 sticks) butter, softened
3 cups sugar
6 eggs
3 cups cake flour, or 2 3/4 cups all-purpose flour
1 cup whipping cream
1 teaspoon vanilla extract

Cream the butter in a mixing bowl. Add the sugar and beat until light and fluffy. Add the eggs one at a time, mixing well after each addition. Add the flour and cream alternately, mixing well after each addition and ending with the flour. Add the vanilla and mix well. Pour into a greased tube pan. Bake at 325 degrees for 1 hour and 20 minutes or until the cake tests done. Cool for 10 minutes in the pan. Remove to a wire rack to cool completely.

Champagne Velvet Cake

Serves 12 to 16

Cake

$2^1/_2$ cups sifted all-purpose flour
$1^1/_2$ cups granulated sugar
1 teaspoon baking soda
1 teaspoon baking cocoa
$^3/_4$ cup plus 2 tablespoons buttermilk
2 eggs
$1^1/_2$ cups vegetable oil
1 teaspoon butternut flavoring
1 teaspoon white vinegar
1 teaspoon vanilla extract
$^1/_4$ cup Champagne

Pecan Cream Cheese Frosting

8 ounces cream cheese, softened
$^1/_2$ cup (1 stick) butter, softened
1 (1-pound) package confectioners' sugar, sifted
2 cups pecans, toasted and chopped
1 teaspoon vanilla extract

To prepare the cake, sift the flour, sugar, baking soda and baking cocoa into a bowl. Add the buttermilk, eggs, oil, butternut flavoring, vinegar, vanilla and Champagne in the order listed, mixing well after each addition. Pour into three greased and floured 8-inch cake pans or two greased and floured 7×11-inch cake pans. Bake at 350 degrees for 30 minutes. Cool in the pans for 10 minutes. Remove to a wire rack to cool completely.

To prepare the frosting, combine the cream cheese and butter in a mixing bowl and beat until well mixed. Add the confectioners' sugar gradually, beating until combined. Stir in the pecans and vanilla. Spread between the layers and over the top and sides of the cooled cake.

Cold Apple Pie

SERVES 6 TO 8

1 1/2 cups pineapple juice
3/4 cup sugar
3 tablespoons cornstarch
1 tablespoon butter
1/4 teaspoon salt
7 apples, peeled and sliced
1/2 teaspoon vanilla extract
1 baked (9-inch) pie shell

Combine the pineapple juice, sugar, cornstarch, butter and salt in a saucepan and bring to a boil, stirring occasionally. Stir in the apples and cook until tender. Remove the apples with a slotted spoon to the pie shell and spread out evenly. Cook the syrup until thickened. Remove from the heat and stir in the vanilla. Pour over the apples. Chill, covered, in the refrigerator until set.

Apple Dumplings

SERVES 8

2 large Granny Smith apples
1 (8-count) can refrigerator crescent rolls
1 cup water
2/3 cup sugar
1/2 cup (1 stick) butter
1 teaspoon vanilla extract
1/2 teaspoon cinnamon

Peel the apples and cut into quarters. Separate the crescent rolls and wrap each apple quarter with a crescent roll. Place seam side down in a baking dish. Combine the water, sugar, butter, vanilla and cinnamon in a saucepan and heat until the butter is melted and the sugar is dissolved, stirring occasionally. Pour over the wrapped apples. Bake at 375 degrees for 30 to 40 minutes or until golden brown. Serve warm with a scoop of vanilla ice cream if desired.

Low-Fat Microwave Chocolate Pie

SERVES 6 TO 8

Our blind parishioner, Carol Holland, developed this recipe and wants people to know it's so easy to make even a blind woman can do it!

1 cup sugar
1/4 cup baking cocoa
1/4 cup cornstarch
Pinch of salt
2 tablespoons butter or margarine, melted
2 eggs
1 (12-ounce) can evaporated skim milk
1/2 cup water
1 1/2 teaspoons vanilla extract
1 (9-inch) graham cracker pie shell
Whipped cream

Combine the sugar, baking cocoa, cornstarch and salt. Place the butter and eggs in a large microwave-safe bowl and blend until smooth. Stir in the dry ingredients until moistened. Combine the evaporated milk and water in a small bowl and mix well. Add to the chocolate mixture and whisk until combined. Microwave on High for 4 minutes. Stir well and return to the microwave. Microwave on High at 1 minutes intervals until the chocolate mixture is thickened and is of pudding consistency, stirring after each interval. Stir in the vanilla. Pour into the pie shell. Chill, covered, for 3 hours. Top with whipped cream before serving.

Pecan Pie

Serves 24

The movie The Grass Harp, *a Truman Capote story, was filmed in Wetumpka in 1994. The incredible cast included Jack Lemmon, Piper Laurie, Walter Matthau, Sissy Spacek, Mary Steenburgen, Nell Carter, Charles Durning, and Roddy McDowell. Walter Mathau's son, Charlie Matthau, was the director. Many of the townspeople enjoyed their roles as extras.*

1/2 cup plus 3 tablespoons butter
1 1/2 cups sugar
6 eggs
3/4 cup corn syrup
3/4 cup Mrs. Butterworth's Syrup
2 teaspoons vanilla extract
Pinch of salt
3 cups chopped pecans
3 unbaked (9-inch) pie shells

Melt the butter in a saucepan over low heat. Add the sugar and stir until well combined. Pour into a large bowl and let stand until cooled. Beat the eggs with a whisk in a bowl until light and frothy. Add to the butter mixture and mix well. Add the corn syrup, Mrs. Butterworth's Syrup, vanilla and salt and mix until combined. Fold in the pecans with a spatula. Pour evenly into the pie shells. Bake at 275 degrees for 1 hour or until the filling is firm and the crust is golden brown.

Praline Pie

SERVES 24

1/2 cup (1 stick) margarine
1 (7-ounce) can flaked coconut
1 cup chopped pecans
1 (14-ounce) can sweetened condensed milk
16 ounces whipped topping
8 ounces cream cheese, softened
3 (9-inch) graham cracker pie shells
Caramel ice cream topping

Melt the margarine in a saucepan. Stir in the coconut and pecans and cook until the coconut browns, stirring frequently. Remove from the heat and let stand until cool. Beat the sweetened condensed milk, whipped topping and cream cheese in a mixing bowl until combined. Divide half the cream cheese mixture evenly among the three pie shells and spread in an even layer. Divide half the pecan mixture among the pie shells and spread an even layer. Drizzle each with caramel topping. Repeat the layers with the remaining ingredients. Cover and freeze for 6 to 8 hours. Let stand to thaw for 5 to 8 minutes before serving.

Mulberry Crisp

Serves 8

In 1900, before Wetumpka had pavement, electric lights, or sewage, mulberry trees grew in the middle of downtown. Few mulberry trees remain, but those who own them cherish them.

4 cups mulberries
Juice of 1 lemon
2 cups all-purpose flour
2 cups sugar
1 cup (2 sticks) butter, softened

Place the mulberries in a buttered 2-quart dish and drizzle with the lemon juice. Combine the flour, sugar and butter in a bowl and mix until crumbly. Sprinkle over the mulberries. Bake at 350 degrees for 45 to 50 minutes or until light brown. Serve warm with vanilla ice cream. (**Note:** *Frozen mulberries may be substituted for the fresh. When using frozen berries, thaw slightly before measuring them so that the measurement is accurate. Blackberries may be used instead of mulberries.*)

Peach Blackberry Cobbler

Serves 8

Peach Blackberry Cobbler is a favorite at Georgia Grille in Atlanta, Georgia. Karen Hilliard, owner and executive chef calls this recipe "hands on" cooking. It has remained on Georgia Grille's menu for sixteen years. It is a perfect partner for ice cream or whipped cream.

2 1/2 cups all-purpose flour
1/2 teaspoon baking soda
1/2 teaspoon salt
1/2 cup shortening
3/4 cup milk
3 cups fresh or frozen blackberries
4 cups fresh or frozen sliced peaches
1/2 cup sugar
1/4 cup (1/2 stick) butter, softened

Combine the flour, baking soda, and salt in a large bowl. Cut in the shortening until crumbly. Add the milk and stir to combine. Turn out onto a floured surface and gently shape the dough into a rectangle that fits in the bottom of a 3-quart baking dish. Layer the blackberries and peaches in the bottom of a 3-quart baking dish. Cover with the pastry. Sprinkle with the sugar and dot with the butter. Bake at 400 degrees for 25 to 30 minutes or until the pastry is golden brown. Serve with ice cream, whipped cream or boiled custard.

Buttermilk Fudge

SERVES 16

2 cups sugar
1 cup buttermilk
1 teaspoon baking soda
1/2 cup (1 stick) butter, softened
2 tablespoons corn syrup
1 cup pecans

Pour the sugar into a 4-quart saucepan. Combine the buttermilk and baking soda in a bowl and add to the sugar. Stir in the butter and corn syrup. Cook, uncovered, over medium heat to 240 to 248 degrees on a candy thermometer, firm-ball stage. Remove from the heat and beat until the mixture thickens and loses its luster. Stir in the pecans. Pour onto a buttered surface or drop by spoonfuls onto a baking sheet. Let stand until firm.

Alabama Pecan Pralines

MAKES 2 DOZEN

1 cup light brown sugar (not packed)
1 cup granulated sugar
1/2 cup evaporated milk
2 tablespoons butter, softened
2 tablespoons white corn syrup
1/16 teaspoon salt
1 3/4 cups pecan halves
1 teaspoon vanilla extract

Place the brown sugar, granulated sugar, evaporated milk, butter, corn syrup and salt in a 2-quart saucepan and stir with a wooden spoon until well combined. Cook, uncovered, over medium-high heat for 10 minute or to 238 degrees, soft-ball stage. Test by dropping a pinch of the mixture into a cup of ice water. The mixture should be soft to the touch but firm enough to roll into a ball between two fingers when removed from the water. Remove the mixture from the heat and stir in the pecans and vanilla. Beat for 1 minute or until the mixture thickens and loses its luster. Drop by teaspoonfuls onto buttered waxed paper. Let stand until firm. Store the candies in an airtight container or wrap.

Almond Snowballs

Makes 2 dozen

1 cup (2 sticks) butter, softened
1/2 cup confectioners' sugar, sifted
1 teaspoon vanilla extract
2 1/4 cups all-purpose flour
1/2 teaspoon salt
3/4 cup ground almonds
Confectioners' sugar

Cream the butter and 1/2 cup confectioners' sugar in a mixing bowl until light and fluffy. Beat in the vanilla. Sift the flour and salt together. Add to the butter mixture and mix well. Stir in the almonds. Shape into walnut-size balls. Place on an ungreased cookie sheet. Bake at 350 degrees for 15 minutes. Roll in confectioners' sugar. Let stand until cool and roll again in confectioners' sugar. (**Note:** *The more times you roll the cookies in the confectioners' sugar, the better the flavor.)*

Macaroons

Makes 25

2 eggs
2/3 cup sugar
4 or 5 tablespoons all-purpose flour
1/2 teaspoon almond extract or vanilla extract
8 ounces flaked coconut

Beat the eggs lightly in a mixing bowl. Add the sugar, flour and almond extract and blend until smooth. Add the coconut and mix well. Drop by spoonfuls onto a well-greased cookie sheet. Bake at 350 degrees for 12 minutes or until light brown. Remove immediately to a wire rack to cool completely. Store in an airtight container. (**Note:** *If the cookies cool on the cookie sheet they will stick.)*

Oatmeal Pecan Cookies

Makes 5 dozen

1/2 cup packed brown sugar
1/2 cup granulated sugar
1/2 cup (1 stick) butter, softened
1/2 cup vegetable oil
1 egg
1/2 teaspoon vanilla extract
1 3/4 cups all-purpose flour
1 teaspoon baking soda
1 teaspoon salt
1 teaspoon cream of tartar
1/2 cup crisp rice cereal
1/2 cup rolled oats
1/2 cup pecan pieces

Cream the brown sugar, granulated sugar, butter and oil in a mixing bowl until light and fluffy. Add the egg and vanilla and blend until combined. Combine the flour, baking soda, salt and cream of tartar and mix well. Add to the sugar mixture and mix until combined. Fold in the cereal, oats and pecans. Shape into balls and arrange on a cookie sheet. Flatten slightly with a glass or by hand. Bake at 350 degrees for 12 to 15 minutes or until golden brown; do not overbake.

Chocolate Pistachio Biscotti

MAKES 10 TO 15

2 cups all-purpose flour
1/2 cup baking cocoa
1 teaspoon baking soda
1/4 teaspoon salt
1 cup sugar
6 tablespoons unsalted butter, softened
2 eggs
1 cup pistachios
1/2 cup (3 ounces) chocolate chips

Combine the flour, baking cocoa, baking soda and salt in a bowl and mix well. Beat the sugar and butter in a mixing bowl until light and fluffy. Add the eggs and mix until smooth, scraping down the side of the bowl as needed. Add the flour mixture and stir until combined, making a firm dough. Stir in the pistachios and chocolate chips. Shape the dough into a slightly flattened 4×12-inch log and arrange on a floured buttered baking sheet. Bake at 350 degrees for 25 minutes or until slightly firm. Cool on the cookie sheet for 5 minutes. Remove to a cutting board. Reduce the oven temperature to 300 degrees. Cut the log on the diagonal with a sharp serrated knife into 1-inch-thick slices. Arrange the slices cut side down on the cookie sheet. Bake for 8 minutes or until crisp but slightly soft in the center. Serve with pistachio ice cream.

Caramel Chocolate Chip Bars

MAKES 2 DOZEN

2 cups all-purpose flour
1 1/2 cups rolled oats
1 cup packed brown sugar
1 cup (2 sticks) butter, softened
1/2 teaspoon salt
1/2 teaspoon baking soda
48 caramels
1/4 cup whipping cream
2 tablespoons all-purpose flour
1 cup (6 ounces) chocolate chips

Mix 2 cups flour, the oats, brown sugar, butter, salt and baking soda in a bowl. Reserve 2 cups for the topping. Press the remaining oat mixture in a 9×13-inch baking pan. Bake at 350 degrees for 10 minutes. Combine the caramels, cream and 2 tablespoons flour in a saucepan and cook until melted and smooth, stirring often. Cool slightly and spread over the baked layer. Sprinkle evenly with the chocolate chips and top with the reserved oat mixture. Bake until the top is light brown. Cool completely before slicing into bars.

The Titus Bluegrass Festival happens on the last Saturday in September and is about the most laid-back, stress-free gathering you'll ever attend. Bring your lawn chair and sit a spell, listening to some good music and eating some good food. The festival supports the Community Center, the former Titus schoolhouse that the Board of Education kindly gave to the community in 1940, but without means of support.

Key Lime Squares

MAKES 35

1 1/2 cups all-purpose flour
3/4 cup (1 1/2 sticks) butter, softened
1/2 cup confectioners' sugar
3 eggs
1 1/2 cups granulated sugar
1/4 teaspoon salt
3 tablespoons all-purpose flour
1/3 cup Key lime juice

Combine the flour, butter and confectioners' sugar in a bowl and mix well. Press in a 9×13-inch baking pan. Bake at 350 degrees for 20 minutes. Beat the eggs lightly in a mixing bowl. Add the granulated sugar and salt and mix until combined. Add the flour and Key lime juice and mix until combined. Pour over the crust, spreading evenly to the edges. Bake for 20 minutes or until set. Remove from the oven and let stand until completely cool. Chill, covered, for 8 to 10 hours before cutting into squares.

Tea Cakes

MAKES 4 DOZEN

1 cup shortening
1 1/2 cups granulated sugar
3 eggs
4 cups all-purpose flour
2 teaspoons baking powder
1 teaspoon baking soda
1/2 teaspoon salt
1/4 cup buttermilk
1 teaspoon vanilla extract
Granulated or decorative sugar for sprinkling (optional)

Cream the shortening in a mixing bowl. Add 1 1/2 cups sugar gradually, beating constantly until light and fluffy. Add the eggs one at a time, mixing well after each addition. Combine the flour, baking powder, baking soda and salt and mix well. Add to the sugar mixture alternately with the buttermilk, mixing well after each addition. Add the vanilla and mix until combined. Chill, covered, for 1 hour. Roll the dough 1/4 inch thick. Cut with a round or a decorative cookie cutter and arrange on a greased cookie sheet. Bake at 350 degrees for 15 minutes or until the edges are golden brown. Sprinkle with additional sugar.

Almond Cheesecake

SERVES 12 TO 16

Crust

1 1/4 cups crushed vanilla wafers
3/4 cup chopped almonds
1/3 cup butter, melted
1/4 cup sugar

Filling

32 ounces cream cheese, softened
1 1/4 cups sugar
4 eggs
1 1/2 teaspoons almond extract
1 teaspoon vanilla extract

Topping

2 cups sour cream
1/4 cup sugar
1 teaspoon vanilla extract
Toasted sliced almonds

To prepare the crust, combine the vanilla wafers, almonds, butter and sugar in a bowl and mix well. Press evenly onto the bottom of a 10-inch springform pan.

To prepare the filling, cream the cream cheese and sugar in a mixing bowl until light and fluffy. Add the eggs one at a time, mixing well after each addition. Add the almond extract and vanilla and beat just until blended. Pour over the crust. Bake at 350 degrees for 55 minutes or until the center is almost set. Cool in the pan for 5 minutes. Maintain the oven temperature.

To prepare the topping, combine the sour cream, sugar and vanilla in a bowl and mix until combined. Spread over the filling. Bake for 5 minutes. Cool completely in the pan on a wire rack. Chill, covered, for 8 to 10 hours. Remove the side of the springform pan. Sprinkle with almonds just before serving.

Angel Custard Dessert

Serves 8

1 envelope unflavored gelatin
1/4 cup cold water
3 egg yolks
1 cup milk
2/3 cup sugar
1 teaspoon vanilla extract
1/2 teaspoon salt
3 egg whites
1/3 cup sugar
1 cup heavy whipping cream
1 angel food cake

Soften the gelatin in the cold water in a bowl and set aside. Whisk the egg yolks, milk and 2/3 cup sugar together in the top of a double boiler. Place over hot water and cook until thickened, whisking constantly. Stir in the vanilla and salt. Stir in the gelatin mixture while the custard is still hot. Let stand until cool. Beat the egg whites in a bowl until frothy. Add 1/3 cup sugar and beat until light and fluffy. Beat the whipping cream in a mixing bowl until firm peaks form. Fold the egg white mixture and whipped cream into the cooled custard. Trim any brown parts from the cake. Pull the remaining cake apart into 1- to 1 1/2-inch pieces. Fold gently into the custard mixture. Spoon into a 7×12-inch baking pan. Chill, covered, for 8 to 10 hours. Serve with whipped cream, one cherry or strawberry and chopped nuts if desired. (**Note:** *This is the perfect dessert to serve for a bridge club or ladies' club group.)*

Crustless Egg Custard

Makes 5 cups

4 eggs
1 3/4 cups sugar
1/2 cup all-purpose flour
1 3/4 cups milk
1 tablespoon vanilla extract
1/4 cup (1/2 stick) butter, melted
Cinnamon

Beat the eggs in a mixing bowl until thick. Combine the sugar and flour in a bowl and mix well. Add gradually to the eggs, beating constantly. Stir in the milk and vanilla. Add the butter and mix until combined. Pour into a greased pie plate and sprinkle with cinnamon. Bake at 325 degrees for 45 minutes or until set. (**Note:** *You may add 3 tablespoons lemon juice, shredded coconut, chocolate chips or anything else desired.)*

Alabama Banana Pudding

Serves 8

3 egg yolks
1 teaspoon vanilla extract
3/4 cup sugar
1/4 cup all-purpose flour
Dash of salt
2 cups milk or half-and-half
Vanilla wafers
2 to 4 bananas, sliced
3 egg whites
6 tablespoons sugar
1/2 teaspoon vanilla extract

Beat the egg yolks in a mixing bowl. Beat in the vanilla. Combine the sugar, flour and salt in a bowl and mix well. Add to the egg mixture and mix until combined. Heat the milk in a large saucepan. Add the egg mixture gradually, whisking constantly until combined. Cook until thickened, whisking constantly. Layer the vanilla wafers and bananas evenly in a baking dish. Top with the pudding. Beat the egg whites in a mixing bowl until frothy. Add the sugar gradually, beating constantly. Add the vanilla and beat until firm peaks form. Spread the meringue over the pudding. Bake at 400 degrees until the meringue is golden brown.

Hot Chocolate Pudding

SERVES 4

2 cups milk
3/4 cup sugar
3 tablespoons baking cocoa
3 tablespoons cornstarch
1/4 teaspoon salt
1/2 teaspoon vanilla extract

Microwave the milk in a 4-cup microwave-safe glass bowl on High for 2 to 3 minutes or until hot. Combine the sugar, baking cocoa, cornstarch and salt in a bowl and mix well. Stir into the hot milk. Microwave on High for 3 to 5 minutes or until smooth and thickened, stirring once or twice. Stir in the vanilla. Spoon into serving dishes and serve warm.

Angel Pie

SERVES 8 TO 10

6 egg whites
1 cup sugar
1/2 teaspoon cream of tartar
1/4 teaspoon salt
1 teaspoon vanilla extract
1 1/2 cups heavy whipping cream
1/2 cup sugar
1/2 teaspoon vanilla
Sliced fresh fruit, such as kiwifruit, strawberries and bananas

Spray a foil-lined non-rimmed baking sheet with nonstick baking spray. Beat the egg whites in a mixing bowl until soft peaks form. Combine 1 cup sugar, the cream of tartar and salt. Beat gradually into the egg whites. Add 1 teaspoon vanilla and beat until firm peaks form. Spoon onto the prepared baking sheet in a 1- to 2-inch-thick circle and smooth the top. Bake at 275 degrees for 1 hour. Turn off the oven, leaving the meringue inside for 30 minutes or until light brown. Remove from the oven and cool completely on the baking sheet. Remove from the foil and place on a serving plate.

Beat the cream in a chilled mixing bowl with chilled beaters until soft peaks form. Add 1/2 cup sugar gradually, beating constantly. Add 1/2 teaspoon vanilla and beat until firm peaks form. Spread over the meringue. Cover with plastic wrap, using wooden picks inserted in the whipped cream mixture to prevent touching. Chill until ready to serve. Arrange fruit in intervals on top just before serving.

Meringues with Lemon Sauce

Serves 4 to 6

Meringues

3 egg whites, at room temperature
1/4 teaspoon cream of tartar
3/4 cup sugar
1 teaspoon vanilla extract

Lemon Sauce and Assembly

3 egg yolks
3/4 cup sugar
1/4 cup (1/2 stick) butter or margarine, melted and cooled
Grated zest of 2 lemons
Juice of 2 lemons
Ice cream
Whipped cream (optional)

To prepare the meringues, beat the egg whites and cream of tartar in a mixing bowl. Add the sugar gradually, beating until combined. Add the vanilla and beat on high speed until stiff peaks form. Spoon four to six mounds of the meringue onto two parchment-lined baking sheets. Spread the mounds into 1-inch-thick circles and make a well with a raised lip in the center of each. Bake at 375 degrees until light brown. Turn off the oven and leave the meringues inside for at least 2 hours; do not open the oven. (**Note:** *You may use one envelope of powdered egg whites instead of making the meringues from scratch. Follow the package directions for making a meringue.)*

To prepare the sauce, combine the egg yolks, sugar, butter, lemon zest and lemon juice in the top of a double boiler and mix until combined. Cook over hot water until thickened, stirring constantly.

To assemble, place each of the meringues on a serving plate. Spoon some sauce into the well and place a scoop of ice cream on top. Drizzle with additional sauce and add a dollop of whipped cream.

Fruit Palette Sauce

Serves 6 to 8

1 1/2 cups fresh or frozen strawberries
1 cup fresh or frozen raspberries
1/2 cup confectioners' sugar
2 tablespoons fresh lemon juice
2 tablespoons Grand Marnier
1/4 teaspoon cinnamon
Sliced fresh seasonal fruit
Sugar cookies or cheese straws
Fresh mint sprigs
Cheese curls

Process the strawberries, raspberries, confectioners' sugar, lemon juice, liqueur and cinnamon in a blender until smooth. Spoon the sauce evenly onto six to eight dessert plates. Arrange fruit decoratively over the sauce. Serve with sugar cookies or cheese straws. Garnish with mint sprigs and cheese curls. (**Note:** *For a beautiful presentation, be sure to include a variety of colors and shapes of fruit, such as bananas, blueberries, grapes, peaches, raspberries, strawberries and tangerines.)*

Amaretto Strawberries

Serves 6 to 8

Strawberries
1/2 cup confectioners' sugar
2 tablespoons amaretto, or to taste
1 pint strawberries

Sauce
8 ounces cream cheese, softened
1/2 cup confectioners' sugar
1 cup sour cream
2 to 4 tablespoons amaretto, or to taste
2 tablespoons cream

To prepare the strawberries, combine the confectioners' sugar and liqueur in a bowl and stir well until blended. Add the strawberries and toss to coat. Spoon the mixture into a sealable plastic bag. Marinate for 4 hours or until ready to serve.

To prepare the sauce, process the cream cheese, confectioners' sugar, sour cream, liqueur and cream in a blender until smooth. Chill, covered, until ready to serve. To assemble, spoon the sauce into stemmed glasses and top with the strawberries.

Perfection Peach Ice Cream

MAKES 1 GALLON

4 pasteurized eggs
1 1/2 cups sugar
6 cups milk
4 cups mashed peeled peaches
1 (14-ounce) can sweetened condensed milk
1 1/2 teaspoons vanilla extract

Beat the eggs in a mixing bowl until light. Add the sugar gradually, beating constantly. Add the milk, peaches, sweetened condensed milk and vanilla and mix well. Pour into an ice cream freezer container. Freeze using the manufacturer's directions.

Lemon Ice Cream

MAKES 3 QUARTS

4 cups half-and-half
3 cups sugar
1 (14-ounce) can sweetened condensed milk
1 cup whipping cream
Juice of 5 lemons

Combine the half-and-half, sugar, sweetened condensed milk, cream and lemon juice in a bowl and mix until combined. Pour into an ice cream freezer container. Freeze using the manufacturer's directions.

Contributors, Recipe Testers, and Committee Members

Lynn Alford
Barrie Aycock,
Glen Ella Springs
Tonia Ayers
Shauna Baker
Mickie Baskett
Rhonda Baughman
Sue Beumer
Jo Dunn Borer
The Butt Brothers
Pat Cannon
Perry Elizabeth Caton
Janette Chalker
Barry Chrietzberg,
Chrietzberg Photography
Julie Crockett
Dee Crokin
Jake Davis
Barbara Davis
Doreen Dickey
Leanne Dickey
Barbara Dreyer
Mary Elizabeth (Ebba) Dunn
Sarah Louise Kendall Dunn
Dr. Julius E. (Beau) Dunn
Jo Farris

Dot Franklin
David Funderburk,
Our Place Cafe
Ann Gibson
Ruth Godwin
Rebecca Gregory
Sandra Griswold
Sandy Hallmark
Jackie Harper
Mark Harris
Susan Hayes
Carol Hickman
Karen Hilliard,
Georgia Grille
Fran Holland
Carol Holland
Judie Hooks
Martha Hosey
Ray Howell
Elise Hughes
Janet Hutto
Dino Jobe
Sandra John
Gloria Johnston
Hazel Jones
Amy Jones

Marceil Joyner
John Keith
Rilla Keith
Virginia Kelly
Katyleene Kendall
Phyllis Kennedy
Charlotte Lackey
Blanche Lamb
Louise Lambert
Harriet Landrum
Voncille Lankford
Linda Law
Virginia Lott
Linda Majors
Sharon Massey
Katy Dunn McCall
Lynda McDanel
Tom McDow
Barbara Meginniss
Paula Kelly Meiners
Bernadette Nickson
Megan Olson
Lucia Penland
Julia Pleus
Teresa Rachal
Belyn Richardson
Alabama's First Lady Patsy Riley
Martha Lee Roberti
Robin Rowe
Sharon Schwartz
Bayne Searcy
Chip Searcy
Dianne Searcy
Pam Stein
Frank Stitt,
Highlands Bar and Grill
Ruth Stovall
Peggy Strength
Jean Therkelsen
Kathy Tracy
Christine Turner
Tina Valier,
Casa Napoli
Leah Vaughan
Rex Vaughan
Nancy Wactor
Sherrell Waddle
Sheila Wade
June Ward
Gene Westbrook
Becky Wilkinson
Cynthia Winkler
David Wium
Leon D. Wium
Suellen Young

THANK YOU ALSO TO THE PARISHIONERS, FAMILY, AND FRIENDS OF TRINITY EPISCOPAL CHURCH WHO HELPED *SHALL WE GATHER* IN COUNTLESS WAYS.

Sponsors

We gratefully acknowledge the following companies
for their generous donations to *Shall We Gather.*

4216 Carmichael Road
Montgomery, AL 36106

Jinright-Turner Insurance & Bonds

PRICE PUBLICATIONS, INC.
THE WETUMPKA HERALD
THE ECLECTIC OBSERVER

300 Green Street • P.O. Box 99
Wetumpka, AL 36092
334-567-7811
Fax: 334-567-3284
www.TheWetumpkaHerald.com
www.TheEclecticObserver.com
Serving Elmore County Since 1898

PrimeSouth
BANK

3936 US Hwy. 231
Wetumpka, AL
334-567-5601
Member FDIC
LOCAL HANDS you've come to know and trust.

Sponsors

We gratefully acknowledge the following companies for their generous donations to *Shall We Gather.*

Serving the River Region
Montgomery • Prattville
Wetumpka
www.riverbankandtrust.com
Member FDIC

1-866-567-0081
www.fcbca.com

Brandt Wright Realty, Inc.

Elmore County Office
194-A Fort Toulouse Road
Wetumpka, AL 36092

Office: 334-514-4949
Fax: 334-514-4475
Toll Free: 877-218-2100

Building quality for America with quality building products and services.
www.jenkinsbrick.com

INDEX

Appetizers. *See also* Dips; Snacks; Spreads
Marinated Roast Beef Sandwiches, 17
Mozzarella Pesto Bites, 16
Pepper Vodka Tomatoes, 12
Pork Tenderloin Sandwiches with Herb Mayonnaise, 17
Tomato, Avocado and Goat Cheese Crostini, 15
Zucchini Cheese Squares, 14

Apple
Apple Dumplings, 164
Apple Spice Cake, 154
Cold Apple Pie, 164

Artichokes
Artichoke and Rice Salad, 44
Brussels Sprouts and Artichoke Casserole, 134
No-Pasta Chicken Casserole, 93
Oyster Artichoke Soup, 36
Ruth Stovall's Chicken Artichoke Casserole, 92

Asparagus
Asparagus with Radish Sauce, 131
Basic Brunch Quiche, 56
Marinated Asparagus, 130

Avocado
Fiesta Chicken Salad, 98
Tomato, Avocado and Goat Cheese Crostini, 15

Beans
Garbanzo Beans with Spinach and Sun-Dried Tomatoes, 133
Green Beans Delectable, 132
Green Beans Dijon, 133
Lemon Dill Green Beans, 132
Red Beans and Rice, 88

Beef. *See also* Ground Beef
Beef Stew, 78
Bessie Brand's Camp Stew, 77
Marinated Roast Beef Sandwiches, 17
Patsy Riley's Vegetable Soup, 32
Pot Roast New Orleans, 75
Roasted Beef Tenderloin Glen Ella, 74
Very Special Brisket, 76

Beverages
Bourbon Slush, 27
Champagne Punch, 28
Limoncello, 29
Limoncello Martini, 29
Spiced Cranberry Cider, 27

Biscuits
Country Ham Sour Cream Biscuits, 63
Garlic Cheese Biscuits, 63

Breads. *See also* Biscuits; Corn Breads; Muffins
Baked French Toast, 62
Crawfish Bread, 65
Italian Pull-Apart Bread, 65
Refrigerator French Bread, 70
Refrigerator Rolls, 71
Rosemary Raisin Walnut Bread, 67
Tidewater Spoon Bread, 66

Cakes
Apple Spice Cake, 154
Bette's Chocolate Sheet Cake, 153
Brown Sugar Pound Cake, 161
Champagne Velvet Cake, 163
Episcopalian Cake, 150
Espresso Chocolate Torte, 151
Jeanette Belcher's Creole Cake, 152
Katyleene Kendall's Gingerbread with Lemon Sauce, 160
Lane Cake, 158
Orange Date Nut Cake, 155
Pineapple Cake, 156
Pumpkin Crunch Cake, 159
Pumpkin Roll, 159
Whipping Cream Pound Cake, 162
White Fruitcake, 157

Candy
Alabama Pecan Pralines, 169
Buttermilk Fudge, 169

Chicken
Baked Chicken, 96
Bessie Brand's Camp Stew, 77

INDEX

Chicken and Sun-Dried Tomatoes, 103
Chicken and Wild Rice, 105
Chicken in Basil Sauce, 94
Chicken Supreme, 104
Chilled Chicken Elise, 95
Easy Chicken Pie, 97
Fiesta Chicken Salad, 98
Grilled Chicken and Peach Salad, 100
Jamaican Chicken Stew, 101
Jumpin' Jambalaya, 120
Maple Chicken Salad, 99
Mediterranean-Style Chicken, 102
No-Pasta Chicken Casserole, 93
Old-Fashioned Chicken Salad, 98
Ruth Stovall's Chicken Artichoke Casserole, 92
Savory Shrimp and Chicken Casserole, 119

Chocolate
Bette's Chocolate Sheet Cake, 153
Caramel Chocolate Chip Bars, 173
Champagne Velvet Cake, 163
Chocolate Pecan Icing, 153
Chocolate Pistachio Biscotti, 172
Espresso Chocolate Torte, 151
Hot Chocolate Pudding, 178
Jeanette Belcher's Creole Cake, 152
Low-Fat Microwave Chocolate Pie, 165

Cookies
Almond Snowballs, 170
Caramel Chocolate Chip Bars, 173
Chocolate Pistachio Biscotti, 172
Key Lime Squares, 173
Macaroons, 170
Oatmeal Pecan Cookies, 171
Tea Cakes, 174

Corn Breads
Cracklin' Corn Bread, 69
Mexican Corn Bread, 69
Wetu Hushpuppies, 69

Crab Meat
Alabama Seafood Gumbo, 121
Crab au Gratin, 108
Hot Crab Dip, 18
Our Place She Crab Soup, 35
Rice and Crab Romanoff, 109
Seafood Royale, 122

Cranberry
Asheville's Cranberry Orange Cheese Ball, 23
Champagne Punch, 28
Spiced Cranberry Cider, 27

Desserts. *See also* Cakes; Candy; Cookies; Pies, Dessert; Sauces, Dessert
Alabama Banana Pudding, 177
Almond Cheesecake, 175
Amaretto Strawberries, 180
Angel Custard Dessert, 176
Angel Pie, 178
Apple Dumplings, 164
Crustless Egg Custard, 177
Hot Chocolate Pudding, 178
Lemon Ice Cream, 181
Meringues with Lemon Sauce, 179
Mulberry Crisp, 168
Peach Blackberry Cobbler, 168
Perfection Peach Ice Cream, 181

Dips
Baked Vidalia Onion Dip, 22
Hot Crab Dip, 18
Monterey Jack and Cheddar Salsa, 25
Peach Salsa, 26
Pickled Black-Eyed Peas, 12
Shrimp Dip, 19
Tomato Salsa, 25

Egg Dishes
Basic Brunch Quiche, 56
Eggs "Bama"-dict, 55
Eggs Florentine Frittata, 54
Potato-Crusted Sausage Quiche, 57
Sausage Egg Soufflé, 59

Eggplant
Caponata, 21
Egyptian Moussaka, 81

Fish. *See also* Salmon
Catfish Croquettes, 123
Coosa Fish Camp Stew, 124
Pan-Fried Tilapia, 125

INDEX

Frostings
Chocolate Pecan Icing, 153
Cream Cheese Frosting, 161
Lane Frosting, 158
Orange Whipped Cream Frosting, 151
Pecan Cream Cheese Frosting, 163

Fruit. *See also* Apple; Avocado; Cranberry; Lemon; Orange; Peach; Pineapple; Pumpkin; Strawberry
White Fruitcake, 157

Grits
Hissy Fit Grits 'n' Greens Casserole, 61
Shrimp and Grits, 60
Zesty Grits Casserole, 59

Ground Beef
Egyptian Moussaka, 81
Hot Texas Chili, 79
Old World Lasagna, 80

Ham
Coca-Cola Ham, 82
Country Ham Sour Cream Biscuits, 63
New Year's Day Soup, 34
Red Beans and Rice, 88

Lemon
Limoncello, 29
Limoncello Martini, 29
Lemon Dill Green Beans, 132
Lemon Ice Cream, 181
Lemon Pesto, 42
Lemon Sauce, 179
Tomato, Lemon and Carrot Soup, 40

Muffins
Cheesy Sausage Muffins, 58
Six-Week Bran Muffins, 64
Sweet Potato Muffins, 64

Okra
Alabama Seafood Gumbo, 121
Boiled Okra, 128
Fried Okra, 128

Onions
Baked Vidalia Onion Dip, 22
Black-Eyed Peas with Tomato and Onion Sauce, 136
Green Tomato and Vidalia Onion Tart, 143
Onion Shortcake, 137

Orange
Asheville's Cranberry Orange Cheese Ball, 23
Orange Date Nut Cake, 155
Orange Whipped Cream Frosting, 151

Oysters
Alabama Seafood Gumbo, 121
Oyster Artichoke Soup, 36
Oysters Rockefeller Casserole, 110
Oysters Saint Louis, 111

Pasta
Angel Hair Pasta with Shrimp and Goat Cheese, 115
Chicken in Basil Sauce, 94
Macaroni and Cheese Deluxe, 147
Old World Lasagna, 80
Pasta Salad with Tomatoes and Peas, 50
Penne Pasta with Shrimp and Squash, 117
Zucchini Pasta Bake, 145

Peach
Grilled Chicken and Peach Salad, 100
Peach Blackberry Cobbler, 168
Peach Salad Dressing, 100
Peach Salsa, 26
Perfection Peach Ice Cream, 181

Peas, 129
Black-Eyed Pea Hummus, 20
Black-Eyed Peas with Tomato and Onion Sauce, 136
Field Pea Casserole, 137
New Year's Day Soup, 34
Pasta Salad with Tomatoes and Peas, 50
Pickled Black-Eyed Peas, 12

Pies, Dessert
Angel Pie, 178
Cold Apple Pie, 164
Low-Fat Microwave Chocolate Pie, 165

INDEX

Pecan Pie, 166
Praline Pie, 167

Pies, Savory
Easy Chicken Pie, 97
Green Tomato and Vidalia Onion Tart, 143
Tomato Pie, 144

Pineapple
Hot Buttered Pineapple, 147
Pineapple Cake, 156

Pork. *See also* Ham; Sausage
Barbecue Pork Ribs, 87
Bessie Brand's Camp Stew, 77
Cracklin' Corn Bread, 69
Kickin' Boston Butt Roast with Jalapeño Coleslaw, 85
Pork Tenderloin Sandwiches with Herb Mayonnaise, 17
Rib Rub, 87
Smokin' Grilled Pork Chops, 84
Traditional Pork Barbecue, 86
Western-Style Pork Chops, 84
Wine-Basted Pork Loin, 83

Potatoes
Potato-Crusted Sausage Quiche, 57
Rosemary Roasted Potatoes with Goat Cheese, 139
Shirley Eberhart's Country Company Potatoes, 138
Tootsie's Potato Salad, 47

Poultry. *See* Chicken

Pumpkin
Pumpkin Chowder, 38
Pumpkin Crunch Cake, 159
Pumpkin Roll, 159

Rice
Alabama Seafood Gumbo, 121
Artichoke and Rice Salad, 44
Chicken and Wild Rice, 105
Jumpin' Jambalaya, 120
Red Beans and Rice, 88
Rice and Crab Romanoff, 109
Seafood Royale, 122
Shrimp and Wild Rice Casserole, 118

Salad Dressings
Caesar Dressing, 114
Creamy Cucumber Dressing, 46
Grandmother's French Dressing, 48
Herb Vinaigrette, 51
Peach Salad Dressing, 100
Poppy Seed Dressing, 50
Strawberry Dressing, 51

Salads
Artichoke and Rice Salad, 44
Bread Salad, 44
Coleslaw with Tomatoes, 45
Grapefruit Aspic Salad with Creamy Cucumber Dressing, 46
Greek Salad, 45
Jalapeño Coleslaw, 85
Pasta Salad with Tomatoes and Peas, 50
Tootsie's Potato Salad, 47
Vegetable Mold, 21
Wilted Spinach Salad, 48
Zippy Tomato Aspic, 49

Salads, Main Dish
Casa Napoli Blackened Shrimp Caesar Salad, 114
Fiesta Chicken Salad, 98
Grilled Chicken and Peach Salad, 100
Maple Chicken Salad, 99
Old-Fashioned Chicken Salad, 98

Salmon
Honey Sesame Salmon Steaks, 125
Smoked Salmon Pâté, 18

Sandwiches
Marinated Roast Beef Sandwiches, 17
Pork Tenderloin Sandwiches with Herb Mayonnaise, 17

Sauces, Dessert
Caramel Sauce, 154
Fruit Palette Sauce, 180
Lemon Sauce, 160, 179

INDEX

Sauces, Savory
First-Place Barbecue Sauce, 89
Green Peppercorn Sauce, 95
Hollandaise Sauce, 55
Horseradish Sauce, 74
Lemon Pesto, 42
Tangy Barbecue Sauce, 89

Sausage
Cheesy Sausage Muffins, 58
Jumpin' Jambalaya, 120
New Year's Day Soup, 34
Old World Lasagna, 80
Potato-Crusted Sausage Quiche, 57
Red Beans and Rice, 88
Sausage and Turnip Green Soup, 33
Sausage Egg Soufflé, 59
Zesty Grits Casserole, 59

Seafood. *See also* Crab Meat; Fish; Oysters; Shrimp
Crawfish Bread, 65

Shrimp
Alabama Seafood Gumbo, 121
Angel Hair Pasta with Shrimp and Goat Cheese, 115
Barbecue Shrimp, 112
Biloxi Boiled Shrimp, 113
Black Pepper Shrimp, 113
Casa Napoli Blackened Shrimp Caesar Salad, 114
Greek Island Shrimp, 116
Jumpin' Jambalaya, 120
Layered Shrimp Party Platter, 19
Penne Pasta with Shrimp and Squash, 117
Savory Shrimp and Chicken Casserole, 119
Seafood Royale, 122
Shrimp and Grits, 60
Shrimp and Wild Rice Casserole, 118
Shrimp Dip, 19

Side Dishes. *See also* Grits; Rice
Hot Buttered Pineapple, 147
Macaroni and Cheese Deluxe, 147
Mama's Dressing, 146

Snacks
Cheese Straws, 13
Party Pecans, 13

Soups. *See also* Stews
Cream of Garlic Soup, 37
Gazpacho, 43
New Year's Day Soup, 34
Our Place She Crab Soup, 35
Oyster Artichoke Soup, 36
Patsy Riley's Vegetable Soup, 32
Pumpkin Chowder, 38
Roasted Red Bell Pepper Soup, 39
Sausage and Turnip Green Soup, 33
Spring Minestrone, 42
Tarragon Tomato Soup, 41
Tomato, Lemon and Carrot Soup, 40

Spinach
Eggs Florentine Frittata, 54
Garbanzo Beans with Spinach and Sun-Dried Tomatoes, 133
Wilted Spinach Salad, 48

Spreads
Asheville's Cranberry Orange Cheese Ball, 23
Black-Eyed Pea Hummus, 20
Caponata, 21
Layered Shrimp Party Platter, 19
Olive and Mushroom Cheese Ball, 23
Smoked Salmon Pâté, 18
Three-Pepper Pimento Cheese, 24
Vegetable Mold, 21
Zesty Cream Cheese, 22

Squash
Penne Pasta with Shrimp and Squash, 117
Summer Squash Casserole, 141

Stews
Alabama Seafood Gumbo, 121
Beef Stew, 78
Bessie Brand's Camp Stew, 77
Coosa Fish Camp Stew, 124
Jamaican Chicken Stew, 101

INDEX

Strawberry
Amaretto Strawberries, 180
Strawberry Dressing, 51

Sweet Potatoes, 129
Rosemary Roasted Sweet Potatoes, 139
Sweet Potato Casserole, 140
Sweet Potato Muffins, 64

Tomatoes
Baked Tomato Slices, 144
Black-Eyed Peas with Tomato and Onion Sauce, 136
Chicken and Sun-Dried Tomatoes, 103
Coleslaw with Tomatoes, 45
Garbanzo Beans with Spinach and Sun-Dried Tomatoes, 133
Green Tomato and Vidalia Onion Tart, 143
Pasta Salad with Tomatoes and Peas, 50
Pepper Vodka Tomatoes, 12
Tarragon Tomato Soup, 41
Tomato, Avocado and Goat Cheese Crostini, 15
Tomato, Lemon and Carrot Soup, 40
Tomato Pie, 144
Tomato Salsa, 25
Zippy Tomato Aspic, 49

Turnip Greens, 129
Sausage and Turnip Green Soup, 33
Turnip Green Casserole, 142

Vegetables. *See also* Artichokes; Asparagus; Beans; Eggplant; Okra; Onions; Peas; Potatoes; Spinach; Squash; Sweet Potatoes; Tomatoes; Turnip Greens; Zucchini
Broccoli with Olive Butter, 134
Butterbeans, 128
Cabbage and Leeks in Cream Sauce, 135

Zucchini
Fiesta Chicken Salad, 98
Penne Pasta with Shrimp and Squash, 117
Zucchini Cheese Squares, 14
Zucchini Pasta Bake, 145

Shall We Gather

RECIPES AND REMEMBRANCES OF A RIVER TOWN

Trinity Episcopal Church
5375 U.S. Highway 231
Wetumpka, Alabama 36092-3168
334-567-7534
www.trinitywetumpka.org/cookbook

Please call, write, or visit our Web page to order additional copies of *Shall We Gather* to share with family and friends.

Please send $22.95 per book plus $4.00 postage and handling for the first book and $2.00 for each additional book shipped to the same address. If shipping to an Illinois address, add $1.84 sales tax per book.

Wholesale prices are available upon request.

Prints of the cover art are available through our Web site.